Sharing Wisdom

A Process for Group Decision Making

Mary Benet McKinney, O.S.B.

A Guide to Being and Building Church

ThomasMore®
– An RCL Company –
Allen, Texas

Acknowledgments

All Scripture quotations, unless otherwise noted, are from *The Jerusalem Bible.* Minor adaptations have been made in some Scripture passages to incorporate more inclusive language.

Excerpts from *Studies in the Spirituality of Jesuits:* John Carroll Futrell, "Communal Discernment: Reflections on Experience," Jules J. Toner, "The Deliberation That Started the Jesuits" and "A Method for Communal Discernment of God's Will." Copyright by American Assistancy Seminar on Jesuit Spirituality. Reprinted with permission.

Excerpts from Claire M. Brissette, *Reflective Living: A Spiritual Approach to Everyday Life.* Reproduced with permission from Affirmation Books, 109 Woodland St., Natick, MA 01760. Copyright 1983 by Claire M. Brissette.

Excerpts from Joan Chittister, "A Feminine Critique of the Peace Pastoral," *Benedictines,* vol. XXXVII, no. 1. Reprinted with permission.

Excerpts from Matthew Fox, *A Spirituality Named Compassion.* Copyright © 1979 (Winston Press). Reprinted with permission of Harper & Row, Publishers.

Excerpts from John Carroll Futrell, "Learning Leadership from Watershed Down," *Human Development,* vol. 3, no. 4. Reproduced with permission from House of Affirmation, 69 Newbury St., Boston, MA 02116. Copyright 1982 by Jesuit Educational Center for Human Development.

Excerpts from *Silent Presence* by Ernest Larkin. Published by Dimension Books, Denville, NJ 07834. Copyright © 1981. Reprinted with permission.

Chuck Lathrop, "In Search of a Round Table," from *A Gentle Presence* by Chuck Lathrop (Washington, D.C.: ADOC, 1977). Reprinted with permission of the author.

Excerpts from *Lumen Gentium* and *Decree on the Apostolate of the Laity,* taken from *The Conciliar and Post Conciliar Documents.* Reproduced with permission of Costello Publishing Co., Inc., Northport, NY.

Excerpt from Richard P. McBrien, *Catholicism.* Copyright © 1980 (Winston Press). Reprinted with permission of Harper & Row, Publishers.

Excerpt from Philip J. Murnion, "Parish Renewal: State(ments) of the Question," *America* (April 24, 1982). Reprinted with permission of the author and America Press, Inc., 106 W. 56th St., New York, NY 10019. © 1982. All rights reserved.

Excerpts from James H. Provost, ed., *Code, Community, Ministry,* © copyright 1983 by Canon Law Society of America, used with permission.

Excerpts from *Called and Gifted: The American Catholic Laity,* © 1980 by the United States Catholic Conference, Washington, D.C., are used with permission.

Book design by Bonnie Baumann
Cover design by Design Office

Copyright 1987, 1998 Thomas More Publishing

Send all inquiries to:

Thomas More®

An RCL Company

200 East Bethany Drive

Allen, Texas 75002-3804

Toll Free   800–888–3065

Fax   800–688–8356

Printed in the United States of America

ISBN 0–88347–365–8

7 8 9 10 11   02 01 00 99 98

CONTENTS

To all the folks—lay, religious, and clergy—
who, with me, have discovered and nurtured
the philosophy of shared wisdom.

INTRODUCTION

Vatican II called the church to renew herself according to the principles of collegiality and to develop collaborative models of shared responsibility with an emphasis on the baptismal rights of all the people of God. This call has brought about incredible change in these past twenty years. We have seen the growth of new structures at both diocesan and parish levels. Diocesan pastoral councils, priests' senates, boards of education, parish councils, and school boards have all been among the attempts to translate the theology of Vatican II into workable models.

Unbelievable amounts of skill, talent, effort, goodwill, determination, and prayer have been involved in these attempts. But at this point in the lived experience of these models, it is possible to make a rather tragic generalization: For many people and parishes, shared decision making in the Catholic church has not worked that well.

Yes, there are councils and boards and senates that are functioning well—providing a sense of collaboration, bringing laity and clergy together to be and to build church, modeling the theology of Vatican II that church is not simply the responsibility of the ordained but, rather, of the baptized. But for every one that does work, my fourteen years of experience all over the country tell me that there are at least as many that do not!

Have we heard the call of the Council correctly? Have we been wise in the implementation of that call?

Yes and no! Our lived experience of the universality of the way the call has been heard and responded to, plus the recently issued revised Code of Canon Law, certainly affirms our reading of a collegial church, sharing the responsibility and recognizing the centrality of the role of the baptized. So we have heard the call correctly. But what of its implementation?

I submit that by taking a secular model of decision making as we know it in government and management models, we have, unwittingly, guaranteed the malfunctioning of these models as church models. The power struggles that are so much a part of the conflict that seems built into councils and boards are, in fact, inherent to a parliamentary model of decision making.

I intend to offer a church model, grounded in the tradition, that allows for the collaboration of all those involved. This model is based on the belief that the presence of the Spirit is in and with those called to be and to build church, that is, those whose lives of growth in holiness allow them to *be* church and whose commitment to ministry calls them to *build* church.

It must be said at the outset that no model will solve all problems, nor is any model the only answer. Much of what I will say about the model I am proposing can, no doubt, be adapted and adjusted to a variety of models, and I would encourage such adaptation and creativity. The being and building of church is a dynamic process and must flow from the lived experience of those committed to that dynamic. Each parish, diocese, religious community, or any decision makers will need to function in a way that is best for them and the people they seek to serve. And that way may well change as other changes take place: personnel, people's needs, and, most importantly, the call of the Spirit.

What I will offer is a model that I find to be true to my understanding of what it means for people to be and to build church while taking responsibility to strengthen and to nourish that church. The model may well be seen by many as being too idealistic. But then, I feel strongly that Jesus' message calls us to the ideal, that he modeled the ideal in His own life, and that the church is about following Jesus.

Since our attempt to follow Jesus is often limited by the reality of our own human frailties and vulnerability, all of which are so much a part of our lived experience, there will always be the struggles, the failures, the need for healing, and, most of all, the potential for growth. Again, that is part of the dynamic! So the model will attempt to deal realistically with human limitations while, at the same time, calling us to graced experiences of church.

This book is meant to be a working tool that can be given to each member of a board, council, team, or staff. While it can be used by any group seeking to move toward a more prayerful, church-oriented approach to decision making, it is also a useful resource for providing ongoing formation and in-service for boards, councils, and staff members at all levels of church: parish, religious community, diocese, and church-related institutions.

To present the model in a useful way, I have divided the material into nine chapters, each followed by a few focus questions. I would recommend using a chapter a month for personal reading and reflection and then devoting a reasonable amount of time at each monthly meeting to discuss the focus questions and their implications. It would facilitate the process if each person would write out responses to the focus questions in preparation for the meeting.

Two appendices are included in the book. The first one is a collection of procedures, reflection activities, and suggestions for processes. These are materials that I have developed over the years as I have worked with groups to bring them to a shared wisdom model. At appropriate places in the text, references are made to Appendix I. Typically it would be the facilitator, the spiritual leader, or the chairperson who would determine if and how these materials are to be used.

Appendix II is meant to supply some of the historical development of the discernment tradition from the early church to our present efforts to translate the concept into this shared wisdom model. It is intended for private reading and reflection for those who seek additional background information.

To understand the model, to accept its implications, and to begin to move toward its implementation is no small task, but I believe it to be possible and really necessary if shared decision making is to become a part of the church's tradition that our generation hands on to the future. While it may seem overwhelming, I prefer to see the task as one filled with hope and pregnant with the Spirit, and as a response to many people of goodwill who genuinely desire to be and to build church!

I invite you, then, to explore with me a shared wisdom model of church!

1

The Call
of Vatican II

In a lot of subtle and many not so subtle ways, the documents of Vatican II call us to a very different understanding of and approach to church than the one many of us were raised and nourished in through the years of our youth and early adulthood. That church belonged primarily to the ordained. It was their responsibility, their vocation, and their challenge to build and create church and then to call us to, and nourish us through, it. And, let me make haste to add, that approach worked for those of us who are now in the process of being and building church, or we would not continue to be involved with church! But the Council broadened the responsibility, and with it the concept, of ownership. We have come to see church not as the prerogative of the ordained alone, but as the responsibility of all the baptized.

In the preface of their book *Let My People Go,* Alvin Lindgren and Norman Shawchuck say it this way:

> Somehow, over the years, the clergy became the dominant force in the decisions and life of the church. The authors believe that in our day, God's Spirit is again saying to the church and its leaders, "Let my people go, that they might serve me."
>
> ... the clergy cannot do the work of the church, nor can they be the church. Neither can the work of the church be done by the clergy utilizing a handful of faithful lay persons as extensions of their ministry. Likewise, in our sophisticated technical society, laity alone cannot do their full-time secular jobs and do the work of the church on a part-time basis without the trained leadership of the clergy. (1)

1

If there is any Council document in which we hear clearly this call of the Spirit, it is in *Lumen Gentium* where we read:

> The pastors, indeed, should recognize and promote the dignity and responsibility of the laity in the church. They should willingly use their prudent advice and confidently assign duties to them in the service of the church, leaving them freedom and scope for acting. Indeed, they should give them the courage to undertake works on their own initiative. They should with paternal love consider attentively in Christ initial moves, suggestions and desires proposed by the laity. Moreover the pastors must respect and recognize the liberty which belongs to all in the terrestrial city.
>
> Many benefits for the church are to be expected from this familiar relationship between the laity and the pastors. The sense of their own responsibility is strengthened in the laity, their zeal is encouraged, they are more ready to unite their energies to the work of their pastors. The latter, helped by the experience of the laity, are in a position to judge more clearly and more appropriately in spiritual as well as in temporal matters. Strengthened by all her members, the church can thus more effectively fulfill her mission for the life of the world. (2)

And so, for almost twenty years now, pastors and people have attempted to translate this call into workable models of church. The result has been the development of shared decision making groups at almost all levels of church ministry. We have parish and diocesan councils and boards. Within these structures we have committees and commissions and task forces. At the administrative level we have team ministry, staff decision making models, faculty senates, and teachers' organizations. In religious communities we have developed broader-based chapter meetings and community councils that are not merely token advisory groups but genuine decision makers.

Such efforts have been graced and honest responses not only to the challenge of *Lumen Gentium* but also to the vision presented in the *Decree on the Apostolate of the Laity*. In their introduction to this document, the fathers of the Council say:

> In its desire to intensify the apostolic activity of the people of God, the council now earnestly turns its thoughts to the Christian laity. Mention has been made in other documents of the laity's special and indispensible role in the mission of the church. Indeed the church can never be without the lay apostolate. . . . Scripture clearly shows how spontaneous and fruitful was this activity in the church's early days.
>
> No less fervent a zeal on the part of lay people is called for today; present circumstances, in fact, demand from them an apostolate infinitely broader and more intense. . . .

The need for this urgent and many-sided apostolate is shown by the manifest action of the Holy Spirit moving lay people today to a deeper and deeper awareness of their responsibility and urging them on everywhere to the service of Christ and the church. (3)

In Chapter 2 of that same document we read:

... the council earnestly exhorts the laity to take a more active part, according to their talents and knowledge and in fidelity to the mind of the church, in the explanation and defense of Christian principles and in the correct application of them to the problems of our times. (4)

Speaking more specifically on how such participation can evolve, Chapter 3 informs us:

The parish offers an understanding example of community apostolate, for it gathers into a unity all the human diversities that are found there and inserts them into the universality of the church. The laity should develop the habit of working in the parish in close union with their priests, of bringing before the ecclesial community their own problems and questions regarding salvation, to examine them together and solve them by general discussion. (5)

It seems undeniable that during these twenty years, this call for the laity to be actively involved in and responsible for church has been the outgrowth of the reading, reflecting upon, and praying about the call of the Spirit through the Council documents. If we have been tempted to wonder about the validity of that reading, the recently published revised Code of Canon Law should be helpful. Canon law has traditionally been an affirmation of the theology of the time translated into behavioral canons.

James H. Provost, Executive Coordinator of the Canon Law Society of America, focuses our attention on this role of the revised Code as a reflection of the Second Vatican Council in his approach to the Code in the society's recently published study, *Code, Community, Ministry.* Provost writes:

When John XXIII called for an "aggiornamento" of the Code of Canon Law twenty-four years ago this year, he saw it as a way of implementing in the practical life of the church the renewal he was inaugurating in the Catholic Church. In many ways the revised Code is remarkably faithful to the decisions of Second Vatican Council, the touchstone of John's renewal.

The revised law provides a common status for all in the church, based on their baptism and directed toward their involvement in the mission of the church. The distinctions of clergy and laity remain, but are placed in a new context. Instead of building the whole legal structure on the differences between clergy and

laity as the 1917 Code did, this revised law begins with the common dignity of all the baptized and puts distinctions in terms of
service and ministry. . . .

The role of lay persons receives increased attention in the
Code, as it did in Vatican II. Their responsibility for spreading the
Gospel in every walk of life is recalled. Their rights to the spiritual
goods of the church, especially the Word of God and the sacraments, form the basis for several innovations in how ministry is to
be structured, and even the variety of persons who may perform
official church ministry. . . .

[The Code] is an attempt to reflect a new way of thinking, that
"new habit of mind" which Paul VI charged the Code Commission
to implement when he set them upon their task at the conclusion
of Vatican II. . . .

A first expression of this new thinking is in the whole understanding of the church which is reflected in the Code. The 1917
Code clearly addressed the church as a monarchy. . . . The revised
Code attempts to take seriously the sense of church as a commun-
ion, a bonding together of people in the Lord and with one another
at various levels of their church experience. . . .

Another expression of the new way of thinking is in the
approach to ministry. Church office is no longer restricted just to
clergy. (6)

Speaking of issues in the Code which may well become problems
for the church in the United States, however, Provost comments that
one such area is

the role of consultative bodies such as priests' councils, diocesan
pastoral councils, and parish councils. The revised Code can be
read as giving the bishop (or pastor at the parish level) a much
more controlling role in these bodies than is congenial to the
American experience. The struggles of the years since the Council to implement what many rightly understood as shared responsibility and a greater role for priests and lay persons in the life of
the church could be lost if the revised Code is not interpreted very
carefully. (7)

Having admitted that possibility, the authors of the various chapters of Provost's book, all canon lawyers, proceed to call us to an understanding of both church and the Code as a process of enabling all
members, according to their own gifts and willingness, to be and to
build church. Pastors are challenged to foster among the laity an
understanding of and involvement in shared responsibility and the
planning that is appropriate for both pastoral action and the mission of
the parish. This is to be done through councils and committees, thus
affirming the direction taken at all levels of church to establish shared
decision models.

Writing about renewal in the church and specifically relating to the Council document on the laity, Sister Joan Chittister observes:

> That the role of the laity in the church was even an issue at Vatican II may be the greatest turning point of the church's modern history. For, in this decree, the lay state in the church began to be described as a vocation. Multiple charisms were reaffirmed and lay members instructed that the believer "has both a right and a duty to use them." Participation rather than passivity became a factor of commitment. From that rationale came the call to responsibility for church organization, for Catholic education and formation programs, for church administration itself. (8)

If the Spirit, speaking through the bishops of the world gathered in that Council twenty years ago, has called us to a shared responsibility and shared decision making models of church, why, then, are we finding it so difficult? There are many possible explanations, including:

- It's very new and we have to learn how to do it.
- We don't all have the skills.
- Roles are not clear.
- Some pastors feel very threatened.
- Some pastors are manipulative.
- Some lay folks are pushy and domineering.
- Some of us want too much to happen too quickly.
- Some of us are fearful that things are changing too rapidly.
- We may be church but we are also very human.

All of the above, in fact, have something to do with the situation we find ourselves in today. And what is that situation?

As I perceive the "state of the church," I can best sum it up by saying that we now have all over the country thousands upon thousands of boards, councils, senates, committees, and commissions. There are some that really do work well. They provide an arena where laity and clergy work together and complement each other, where they have figured out their roles and the complementarity of these roles. People in these groups feel called to be and to build church, and recognize that call as a call to deepen their own spirituality while attempting to build that part of church they call parish or diocese or community. Growth is evident. Good things are happening. Answers are easier to come by than they were just three or four years ago.

That's the good news. The bad news is that for every one of these models that can be found working well and efficiently and that can be recognized as church, there is at least another one, if not many others, that does not work well, is not efficient, and seems to be anything but church.

The problems brought on by shared decision models are enormous. The disenchantment that all too many pastors and lay people are experiencing is debilitating, frustrating, and in some situations even scandalous. If there is one universal comment I hear as I move around the country, it is the one made by good people at all levels of church structure: "Why must we fight?"

Monthly meetings for many have become battlegrounds. Win-lose struggles create enemies or, at least, cool relationships rather than strengthening them. Far from building church, these models have all too often destroyed it. Clergy and laity have locked themselves into corners that they may never be able to get out of! Neighbors have become combatants in power struggles that threaten to destroy relationships that have managed to survive years of complaints and arguments about noisy parties, children's destruction of property, and even territorial rights of family pets!

A few years ago, when I first allowed myself to admit, at least in the secrecy of my heart and head, that shared decision in church seemed to be creating more problems than it was solving, I began asking myself, and then folks all around the country, "Why isn't it working?" I got some interesting, but not too helpful, answers. They went like this:

- It was never supposed to work.
- Let me show you where it does work.
- Told you so!
- Give it another two or three years.
- Teach us more skills and it will work.
- Pray more prayers with us and it will work.

Well, I kept pushing my question, inviting people to reflect with me on their lived experience and then reflecting back to them some of the insights that began to surface. Little by little it became clear that the problem was not so much in our efforts or even in our human limitations as it was in the model we had attempted to adapt.

What was that model and where had it come from?

It was a parliamentary model that grew out of our experience of how groups make decisions. Early on, most of us learned group decision making in a parliamentary model. In government, business groups, civic and community organizations, and even in social organizations, we dusted off Robert's Rules when decisions had to be made by the group. And, for the most part, it worked. We ended up with a decision that was at least agreed upon by the majority and accepted, more or less, by all.

By its very nature, however, a parliamentary approach to decision making sets up a win-lose posture. It guarantees the power struggles that cause us so much anxiety and frustration in our councils and boards. Consider how we approach our role in a discussion that is being conducted by the use of Robert's Rules.

- We study the agenda items and attempt to analyze our understanding and feelings about them.
- We determine the position we will take on each of the items, or at least on those that are important to us.
- We go to the meeting prepared to so explain, argue, charm, whatever, in order to convince the other members of the group that our reading and analysis is the one that should be adopted.
- We usually listen to others' analysis and arguments not so much to learn from what they have to say as to refute what they have to offer and so bring them over to our way of thinking.
- If, in fact, we succeed in this effort, we have won, we have gained the power and the control. And all we need to do that is one vote over 50 percent of the total membership present and voting.

See what is happening? The power struggles are built in. The efforts to control are just part of the approach. The desire to win is taken for granted, as is the fact that since some people will win, others will lose.

So, what's so bad about that? People often remind me that life is about winning and losing: "You win a few, you lose a few. Why, I even teach my children to be good losers!"

Do you really? Of course not. We try to teach our children how to accept losing, how not to be emotionally undone by the experience. But what parent or teacher or coach ever says to a child, "This is how to lose!" We first teach our children to win and then only what to do if they should be so unfortunate, unclever, unprepared, or unsuccessful as to lose. But the clear lesson is always that it's better to win, so: "Go for it!"

This attitude may, indeed, have its place and be justifiable in some areas of life. (I must admit that I am coming to doubt that, and so are a lot of other people. The reality of this attitude is becoming more obvious in many of the new management models that are being developed by industry today.) What I am more and more convinced of is that this secular model is, in fact, not fully congruent with church, with Gospel values, with the teachings of Jesus, and with the call of the Council!

Let me say it again: Our problem is not that we have misread the call of the Council. It is not in our efforts to develop shared decision models of church. It is not in the lack of goodwill on the part of the people involved, nor is it that we have failed to teach skills. And it certainly is not for lack of prayer and reflection.

What we have done for these past twenty years is attempt to baptize a secular model of decision making. My experience and my reflection on that experience tell me that the model has simply refused baptism! The saving waters have refused to take! We have tried to bookend our meetings with prayer, but that hasn't worked too well, either. Our meetings still tend to erupt in the middle!

Over the last few years, then, I have taken the position that what we must do is either create a new model that will truly be a church model, or find such a model in the tradition and develop it to meet our needs. The result of my seeking has become a combination of the two: a model that has its roots in the early tradition of the church but is adapted and adjusted to respond to the needs and demands of the time. It is a model based on what I have come to call the philosophy of shared wisdom, and it flows from the tradition in the church known as discernment.

Focus Questions for Chapter 1

Answer the following questions to help you prepare for a discussion of them at your next meeting.

1. Explore your personal experience of church before and since Vatican II.

   What are the differences? _____

   _____

   _____

   _____

   What is your understanding of the call and the responsibility of the laity in today's church?

   _____

   _____

   _____

2. Reflect on your experience of shared decision making in church (board, council, staff, etc.).

   What has worked? _____

   _____

   _____

   _____

   What has been difficult or painful? _____

   _____

   _____

   _____

   Has competition, power, and the need to win been part of your experience? If so, how has it affected the group and the process?

   _____

   _____

   _____

3. What are some of the possible implications for you and your group as you consider these questions and the material in Chapter 1?

   _____

   _____

The God
of the Gathering

A model of church built on the philosophy of shared wisdom has strong scriptural support. The basic concept upon which the model rests is the presence of the Spirit in the very lives of the people involved and therefore in the functioning of the group. In Matthew 18:20 Jesus tells us:

> For where two or three meet in my name, I shall be there with them!

We can hear Jesus saying to us through these words:

> When you come together to pray, I shall be with you.
> When you come together to break bread, I shall be with you.
> When you come together to be and to build church, I shall be with you.

Too many of us remember a translation that gave us a visual image that has proven less than helpful. It went like this:

> When two or three are gathered in my name, there I am in the midst of you.

The problem phrase was "in the midst of you." The visual image was of this invisible presence that was somehow right in the middle of the room in which we gathered. Such an image missed the point. Far more intimate is the promise of our God! He will not simply be in the room with us. He will live in our very beings—calling, forming, challenging, speaking, listening. Or, to put it another way, He will be using our ears,

11

our voices, our minds and hearts to be His presence in and for His church.

Jesus Himself promised us such identity, such intimacy, when He said to His followers:

> And know that I am with you always.
> *Matthew 28:20*

And, as His words are recorded from the Last Supper, He provides us with an insight that is critical to our understanding of this promise. In John's Gospel we read:

> I will not leave you orphans; I will come back to you. . . .
> If you love me you will keep my word, and my Father will love you, and we shall come to you. . . .
> The Advocate, the Holy Spirit, whom the Father will send in my name, will teach you everything.   *John 14:18, 23, 26*

So, Jesus came back. But the Gospel stories that follow the resurrection event clearly indicate that He did not come back as His followers had expected. So different was He, in fact, that they did not even recognize Him!

Reflect on those stories and you find a grieving Mary, a woman who loved Jesus deeply, knew Him intimately. Yet when she encountered Him in the garden, she did not know who He was! The little group of travelers on the road to Emmaus had the same problem. All they could think about or talk about was their sense of loss and disappointment over this man they had come to love and respect, this man they had worked with, lived with, celebrated with, struggled with for three years. Few people knew Jesus as well as they did. But they did not know Him as He walked the journey with them.

All the post-resurrection stories have this same theme. Why? Because the Risen Lord had taken on a new way of being present to His people. He *was* the gardener. He *was* the stranger. He was teaching and showing them and us what Scripture scholar Eugene LaVerdiere says this way: "The greatest presence of the Risen Lord is another human being."

The Lord Jesus has not left us orphans! Indeed, He has returned. Through the presence of the Spirit in our lives and in the lives of one another, the Risen Lord calls, forms, challenges, affirms, speaks, listens, lives!

Our God is the God of the Gathering.

True, we find God in Scripture, in Eucharist and sacrament. But we also find this God of ours within our very lives and within the lives of one another—present in the gathering as we strive to be and to build church, present in our council and board meetings, present in team and staff and faculty members.

Which takes us back to a philosophy of shared wisdom. What is it and how does it work?

If we believe the words of Jesus that He will be with us when we gather in His name, and if we understand that presence as being the very presence of the Spirit in each one of us, we can draw some conclusions that will clarify what goes on in a shared wisdom model of church.

As we come together as council, board, senate, team, or whatever, the Spirit, in order to share with us the very wisdom of God, promises to each of us a piece of the wisdom. Repeat: a piece! No one can contain all the wisdom of God, for that would be to be God. However, the Spirit desires to share as much of the wisdom as the group can handle at any given time. To do this, different pieces of that wisdom will be given to different folks.

If we could just keep this clear and operative in our behaviors, many difficulties could be avoided. For example, those of us who tend to think that, in fact, we do have all the wisdom would come to recognize the fallacy of our messiahship. In so doing we would relax and learn to really listen to the wisdom of others. And those of us who find it difficult to accept another's idea if it does not at least complement our own thinking would learn to avoid this common scenario:

> I'm listening to Joe speak and I don't especially like or agree with what he is saying, so I find myself thinking, "I wonder why the Spirit isn't talking to Joe."

Then there are those of us who tend to think that we have little if anything to offer. We would come to trust the value of that wisdom that comes from our own lived experience.

To say that we each have a piece of the wisdom is to say the following:

1. No one has all the wisdom.
Translate: No one knows everything there is to know, regardless of how educated or uneducated, involved or uninvolved, experienced or inexperienced, responsible or irresponsible that person happens to be.

2. Everyone has a different piece.
Translate: Everyone will not agree. In fact, there will be a wide variety of differences and insights.

3. Everyone has some of the wisdom.
Translate: No matter how strange or even "off the wall" a speaker's wisdom may seem, in the midst of it there is something the Spirit is calling the group to consider and, therefore, to listen to, respect, and even treasure.

The bottom line of the philosophy of shared wisdom is a deep and operational faith that the Spirit lives in the group through its membership and speaks through the lived experience of each one. To the degree that the group has both the faith and the skill to surface all the pieces of wisdom that result from this presence of the Spirit, to that degree will the group be able to come up with a decision that reflects the wisdom of the Spirit, the will of God for this group at this time.

Difficult? You bet!

Time consuming? Indeed!

Possible? Not only possible, but at this point in the implementation of the Vatican Council, I see the use of the shared wisdom model as the only way that most of us will ever be able to share decisions in such a way that we create church!

True, some groups have found ways to retain the basic parliamentary structure while so adapting it as to allow for a great deal of what I call shared wisdom. But in my experience, the learned attitudes and the lived experience of this secular model cause it to create unnecessary problems and difficulties. It is out of this experience that I recommend the development of this new model.

This approach to decision making is not new. It has its roots firmly planted in the tradition. In the Acts of the Apostles (chapter 15), we find the story of the council of Jerusalem. Reading this account we recognize an approach to decision making that was collaborative. Peter called the assembly together and allowed all the wisdom to surface before making a final pronouncement that obviously was the result of the shared wisdom and the lived experience of all those involved. Then, as far back as the second century we find an approach to spiritual growth and decision making called discernment. It was recognized as a gift of the Spirit that could be traced through the stories of God's interaction with His people in both the Old and the New Testament.

It is my conviction that the gift of discernment is precisely what we are seeking in our efforts to become decision makers in church. But the tradition is very complicated and deals almost exclusively with the experiences of hermits and cloistered religious in their efforts to discover the will of the Lord in their spiritual journeying. As such, it is impractical and, at first reflection at least, impossible to do for the vast majority of us.

It seems to me, however, that a gift of the Spirit cannot be restricted by life-style, social realities, or place in human history. The challenge, then, is to translate the tradition into a workable model of today's church.

The longer I work at this, study the tradition as found in the sources, and continue my prayerful reflection and the dialogue with others who are attempting the model, the clearer it becomes that more than anything else this model is a call to personal holiness out of which can flow the being and building of church. For years I have intuitively defined the call to serve on boards and councils as not just a call to ministry, but also a call to depth spirituality. I have consistently used the phrase "being and building church." It is now becoming clearer and clearer that "to be church" is, in fact, to strive to be holy!

If there is any single position that stands out in the tradition, it is this call to holiness. I will deal with that in Chapter 3, but first I need to make some observations that will, I believe, provide a frame of reference within which to proceed.

There have been two consistent concerns voiced by people who have been attempting to develop this model with me. Be it a parish council, a diocesan staff, a parish or diocesan board, a team, or a religious community, the "worry list" is the same, namely:

1. It takes so much time.
2. It is so complicated.

Both of these observations tend, indeed, to be true—so true, that one of my major challenges in developing the model is to simplify the process so that it is workable and much less time consuming than people fear it will be or have found it to be. Both of these objectives, I believe, are possible.

But the question I raise is even more important to me and needs far greater development if such a model is to become operational. Is it possible that our resistance to this approach to decision making in church has less to do with our concern about time and complicated procedures and more to do with our instinctive fear that the cost of surrendering ourselves to such depth spirituality will be too great? Is it possible that, as ordinary lay people, we find it hard to believe that the Lord would even call us to such holiness? Or, as pastoral leaders, do we lack the conviction that the Council clearly proclaimed a universal call to holiness? Or is it, perhaps, that as the spiritual leaders of our people, we are not confident enough of our own holiness, our own ability to lead our people on this radical journey of total surrender to the action of the living God in their lives and in ours?

Before even attempting to reflect on these questions it will be helpful to briefly explore the tradition of discernment in the church (the process is fully discussed in Appendix II). From this exploration and reflection, then, it will be possible to draw some implications for its use in our time, thus making it clearer how such a model of church is a response to the call of the Council and is, in fact, a way to be and to build church in twentieth-century America!

Among the many definitions used for discernment, the most common is: "a graced ability." Ernest Larkin speaks of an experience of the indwelling God, a gift that represents "considerable growth and expertise in the life of the Spirit." (1)

It is quite obvious that we are not considering just a structural process for decision making! What we have in this model is a call that touches life in its deepest and most intimate places. It is a call to be in relationship with the Lord; a call to respond to the Spirit who speaks in our hearts and through our lives; a call to believe in the God of the Gathering, the God who speaks to us in and through one another.

Discernment is a gift, albeit a "neglected gift" according to many scholars. As such we find numerous scriptural passages that refer to this active presence of the Spirit within us—this Spirit who makes it possible for us, and even expected of us, to prophesy and discern not only the presence of God in our lives but also the meaning of that presence.

> For this law that I enjoin on you today is not beyond your strength or beyond your reach. It is not in heaven, so that you need to wonder, "Who will go up to heaven for us and bring it down to us, so that we may hear it and keep it?" Nor is it beyond the seas, so that you need to wonder, "Who will cross the seas for us and bring it back to us, so that we may hear it and keep it?" No, the Word is very near to you, it is in your mouth and in your heart for your observance. *Deuteronomy 30:11-14*

> One may have the gift of preaching with wisdom given by the Spirit; another may have the gift of preaching instruction given by the same Spirit; and another the gift of faith given by the same Spirit; . . . one, the power of miracles; another, prophecy; another the gift of recognizing spirits; another the gift of tongues and another the ability to interpret them. *1 Corinthians 12:8-10*

> Never try to suppress the Spirit or treat the gift of prophecy with contempt; think before you do anything—hold on to what is good and avoid every form of evil. *1 Thessalonians 5:19-22*

> But you have been anointed by the Holy One, and have all received the knowledge. *1 John 2:20*

> But you have not lost the anointing that He gave you, and you do not need anyone to teach you; the anointing He gave teaches you everything; you are anointed with truth, not with a lie, and as it has taught you, so you must stay in Him. *1 John 2:27*

Both scholarly research and prayerful reflection lead us to realize that the gift of discernment is not something given only to a very few. It is not some mysteriously mystic experience or calling. Rather, "You have been anointed . . ." It is part of the call to be Christian. It is the result of the presence of the Lord in our lives, the gift of the Spirit given us at baptism. It is a call to holiness.

This call to holiness is, in the final analysis, a call to contemplation. Larkin, in his book *Silent Presence,* says it clearly when he writes:

> Contemplation and personal discernment are recognized today as normal developments in the spiritual life. Both are experiences of the indwelling God; they are gifts that represent considerable growth and expertise in the life of the Spirit. . . .
>
> Contemplation and discernment deal directly with the mysterious, incomprehensible God who appears among us and is experienced in Himself (contemplation) or in a given human situation (discernment). Discernment asks us to be contemplatives in action, in our human choices, finding the same God outside whom we discover in silent prayer. . . .
>
> . . . discernment should not be regarded as a litmus test, to be applied at key moments of decision. It is spirituality in the concrete, because spirituality is precisely the Spirit *acting* within us and discernment is the awareness of that action.
>
> Spirituality has long suffered from being identified as theory to be applied; it is life first and only then a reflection on life. It is *experiencing* with understanding and commitment the presence and guidance of God in one's whole life. That is discernment, too. Discernment is thus a life work. (2)

It is quite possible to discern the will of God, even with a great deal of clarity, and then say, "No thank you!" Central, then, to this approach to spiritual growth is what is identified in the tradition as interior freedom, purity of heart, indifference, or disinterestedness. This ability to "let go" is critical if the discerner is to be able not only to hear what the Spirit is revealing but also to respond with the appropriate action.

Imperative to the model, then, is the ongoing struggle to "let go" in the sense of allowing God to be God in our lives and in our church. It is this outgrowth of spirituality that seems most clearly to place the decision-making process in its proper perspective. This part of the tradition will need to be preserved in any adaptation of that tradition. For most of us, "letting go" will probably be a lifelong struggle and challenge! It is never easy to "let go" of our own wisdom. It is the unusual person who does not tend to favor his or her own opinions. This is especially true of people who see themselves as having the skills, the experience, and the call to be decision makers!

Yet it is, I believe, precisely this kind of "holy indifference," this ability to "let go" and seek the will of the Spirit in the gathered wisdom rather than in the wisdom of any one individual, that is the challenge of this model. Just as none of us can be church alone, so none of us can hear the total wisdom of the Spirit alone. We need each other; we need to surrender to the God of the Gathering.

Focus Questions for Chapter 2

Answer the following questions to help you prepare for a discussion of them at your next meeting.

1. Reflect on your experience of the God of the Gathering. How have you met this God—

in family? _____

_____

_____

in church? _____

_____

_____

in life?_____

_____

_____

_____

2. Consider this statement: "No one has all the wisdom."

What behaviors model that conviction? _____

_____

_____

What behaviors belie it? _____

_____

_____

3. What would help you and your group to be more in touch with the God of the Gathering?

_____

_____

_____

3

Spirituality

A call to participate in a shared decision model of church is, it seems to me, a call to ministry and a call to spirituality. The call to ministry challenges me to accept responsibility for the nourishing and strengthening of church. The call to spirituality challenges me to develop a relationship with God that results in a deepening intimacy with the Lord and enables me to grow in that difficult "letting go" stance. I grow to recognize the presence of the Spirit in my life. I grow to trust the working of the Spirit in the experiences of my life. It is a call to process life, a call to contemplation. For it is not possible for me to hear the God of the Gathering if I am not in touch with the God of my own lived experience.

In November of 1980 the National Council of Catholic Bishops issued a statement entitled *Called and Gifted: The American Catholic Laity.* It represented the reflections of the American bishops on the role of the laity, and commemorated the fifteenth anniversary of the issuance of the *Decree on the Apostolate of the Laity.* In it the bishops state:

> The Second Vatican Council clearly proclaimed the univer-
> sal call to holiness. Not only are lay people included in God's call
> to holiness, but theirs is a unique call requiring a unique response
> which itself is a gift of the Holy Spirit. It is characteristic that lay
> men and women hear the call to holiness in the very web of their
> existence (*Lumen Gentium,* 31), in and through the events of the
> world, the pluralism of modern living, the complex decisions and
> conflicting values they must struggle with, the richness and fragility

19

of sexual relationships, the delicate balance between activity and stillness, presence and privacy, love and loss.

The response of lay people to this call promises to contribute still more to the spiritual heritage of the Church. Already the laity's hunger for God's word is everywhere evident. Increasingly lay men and women are seeking spiritual formation and direction in deep ways of prayer. This has helped to spur several renewal movements. (1)

And I would add to the bishops' wisdom: It has also helped to make possible the development of boards and councils that are genuine church models. For it is only out of a deep and personal spirituality, a growing awareness of the Lord speaking in my life, that I can surrender to the Spirit in the group, sharing my wisdom and treasuring the wisdom of others.

This seeking for the Lord in new and intimate ways on the part of the laity has been for me one of the major indicators that we are being called to this kind of a model. The management models we have tried to develop simply fall short of the hopes and expectations of so many people as they grow in their awareness of what church can be and what part they might be able to play in the formation of that church. People are seeking holiness. They are seeking a church that calls them to holiness, a church that reflects Gospel values, not just in its worship and sacramental system, but in its response to social issues, in its care for people, and, yes, in the way it goes about determining priorities and making decisions. The Spirit is already moving over this country, calling, forming, challenging, preparing folks to be and to build church in the light of Vatican II!

The spirituality called for in this shared wisdom model is built on the Judeo-Christian tradition that our God is a personal God, a God who cares, a God who inserts Himself into our very lives. Such a God is always and everywhere present in and to us. It is we who are sometimes absent.

The holiness called for, then, is a holiness that puts us in touch with this God who lives life with us. It is a holiness that teaches us to be in touch with our lived experience.

What other kind of experience is there, you ask? What else is experience if it is not lived? How about muddled through? Or ignored? My experience tells me that it is quite possible to live large portions of life on automatic. I wake up in the morning, push the On button, and move through the day, often on Fast Forward, until night comes. Then I collapse in a heap, push the Off button, and am grateful for having made it through another day. I've survived but I've not lived my experience. I've failed to ask the once-famous quotation: "What's it all about, Alfie?"

In her recently published book *Reflective Living,* Claire Brissette speaks to this reality in so many of our lives. She writes:

> To some extent, each of us tends to live in a state of wakeful sleep, more or less consciously going through the motions of our everyday life and experience. Rarely do we take the time to get in touch with and to reflect upon the deeper meanings of our experiences. We tend to feel that such reflection is simply a waste of time.
>
> Yet the potential for reflection is rooted in our nature. Each of us has the ability to touch the deeper meanings of our everyday experience. Through reflection we glimpse something of the mystery of life, and as a consequence our lives are enriched. Daily activity ceases to be monotonous, and reflective dwelling opens our eyes to the wonder hidden in the most insignificant experiences. (2)

In the chapter on "Developing a Reflective Approach to Daily Life," Brissette observes:

> The common ways of Christian living such as personal prayer, periods of silence and solitude, spiritual reading, and retreat are time-tested structures that foster within us growth in a reflective attitude. They lead us toward a deepened relationship with God. However, it is not sufficient that these common ways be highly encouraged by the Church. . . . Nor is it enough for us to know that we need silence and solitude, prayer and reconciliation. In order to be effective, these common ways must become our own. We need to create the space for them in the here and now of our daily lives.
>
> . . . just as human love needs to be nurtured if it is to grow, so too does our relationship with God require nourishment. The common ways of Christian living constantly remind us of our call to incorporate these structures into our lives in a way that is realistically possible. (3)

To live my experience, to allow the Spirit who dwells within my very being to touch and to form me, I need to process my life daily. Again, my experience tells me that while we will do this according to our personalities and life-styles, three things are necessary if we are to really touch and learn from our daily lives. They are a serious commitment to—

- prime time,
- God space,
- an appropriate method.

Allow me to speak to each of these. First there is prime time. To process life, I need some time each day with the Lord to discuss the "what's it about" question. It does not usually take a lot of time, perhaps only fifteen or twenty minutes on most days. But it needs to be *prime* time, not leftover time when my head has already turned off. Prime time will be different for different folks. Some of us are morning people. When we wake up, we really wake up! We are ready to take the world on from the moment we leap out of bed. For us, prime time is early morning. Others among us can hardly find our world as we painfully crawl out of bed. We come alive much later in the day and are really into life as the sun begins to set. We are night people. The point is, prime time for me is that time of the day or night when my head works best—when I am most alert, most awake, most productive. It is fifteen or twenty minutes of that time the Lord asks of me *each* day.

Then there is God space. And what is that? A place of solitude. A place where I will not be disturbed by child, phone, dog, or whatever. Such a place is not easy to come by but not impossible if I work at it. It may be my bedroom or some place outside where I can walk or sit. It may be a church or chapel. For many who drive a lot, it may be the car. Some folks tell me it's the bathroom! Where it is, is not important. What's important is that it provides privacy, a space in which to be alone with my God.

And finally there is an appropriate method. How am I to do this thing called processing life? How do I go about asking the Lord what the day has been about? Most importantly, I go about it in a way that is possible, comfortable, and productive for me. To process life is to do two things: (1) ask the Lord some questions about the events of the day, the people who came into my life, and my reactions, feelings, failings, and so on, and (2) listen for His response. This is a call to communicate with God—a call to allow my God to touch me, call me, challenge me, affirm me, meet me in the very depths of my being. It is, I believe, a call to contemplation.

Many of us have very strange notions about contemplation. These notions usually start with the conviction that contemplation is something that someone else does. Great saints and mystics contemplate, not ordinary folk like me. Not so! Contemplation is attentiveness to the experience of the love of God in one's life. It is asking and then hearing the answer to such questions as, How did you touch me today, Lord? What was all the frustration of this day about, Lord? Why did you let me fail, Lord? What were you telling me in the joy and the laughter of this day, Lord? What are you showing me in my experience of being so loved and cherished, Lord?

But how do you *do* it? Again, I think we get lost in our images of contemplatives as being apart, different, or even a bit strange. I spent many years of my life believing that I would never be contemplative even though I intuitively felt a call to that depth of spirituality. But somehow I had gotten the notion that to contemplate was simply to allow oneself *to be* in the presence of the Lord. You were not *to do* anything. Well, just being is not my gift. I am a doer. Or, to put it another way, I'm an extrovert. So what has that *to do* with contemplation? Quite a bit, I've discovered.

Interestingly enough, that simple distinction between extroverts and introverts has important ramifications for contemplation, for this processing of life. Introverts are people who live within themselves. They think while they think. Their world of thoughts and ideas is within their very beings. Extroverts are not like that. We live outside of ourselves. We do not think when we think; we think when we talk, which, by the way, is why we talk so much! Our world of thoughts and ideas exists where we can see and hear and touch them.

Translate this to processing life and it begins to make sense that different people will need to do it in different ways. Introverts can sit quietly in the presence of God. In the depths of their being they can communicate with the Spirit, asking questions, listening to the answers, and drawing the conclusions without ever verbalizing anything. Extroverts find this very difficult if not impossible to accomplish in this manner. We need to speak *out loud* or to write our conversations with the Lord. Extroverts, for example, usually find it very helpful to keep spiritual journals. They talk to themselves while driving the car or jogging around the block or when they are alone at home or anyplace, for that matter. And, for them, that may well be the most workable and effective way to contemplate.

My point: Do what works for you! Talk. Write. Think. Sit still. Walk around. Kneel. Sit. Stand. Go for a ride. Take the dog for a run. The important thing is not *how* to do it. The important thing is *to do it!* I must touch the God of my daily experience and allow the Spirit to speak to me through that experience. This is to live life.

It is only, I submit, as we are willing to accept this call to depth spirituality that we will be able to function in a model of church that flows from the philosophy of shared wisdom. It is only as I come to recognize, respect, marvel at, and be open to the Spirit in my life that I can recognize, respect, marvel at, and be open to the God of the Gathering, the Spirit living in the lives and experiences of those gathered around the decision-making tables of parishes, dioceses, and religious communities.

The challenge of this model is great, perhaps overwhelming. Anything that asks holiness of us tends to overwhelm us! It calls not only for great commitment but also for deep faith. Especially does it challenge us to believe in the presence of the Spirit to us as we seek to be and to build church.

One of the most comforting scriptural passages for me, as I struggle with this call to believe and to trust, is found in the Book of Wisdom.

The Scripture scholars tell us that in this book the word *wisdom* is used to refer to the Spirit. Listen, then, to what the Lord Yahweh says to us in the sixth chapter of that book:

> Wisdom is bright, and she does not grow dim.
> By those who love her she is readily seen,
> and found by those who look for her.
> Quick to anticipate those who desire her,
> she makes herself known to them.
> Watch for her early and you will have no trouble;
> you will find her sitting at your gates.
> Even to think about her is understanding fully grown;
> be on the alert for her and anxiety will quickly leave you.
> She herself walks about looking for those who are worthy of her
> and graciously shows herself to them as they go,
> in every thought of theirs coming to meet them.
>
> *Wisdom 6:12–17*

As I reflect on that passage I hear the Spirit calling to us, tenderly, gently, lovingly, and challenging us to believe and to take courage in that belief. Hear with me, then, as I paraphrase this quote from Wisdom, the Spirit speaking to all of us who commit ourselves to shared responsibility and shared decision making in church—to all of us who gather around the meeting tables of our parishes and dioceses and communities.

> I, Wisdom, am with you.
> I am a light that will never grow dim.
> Love me and you will see me.
> Look for me and you will find me.
> In fact, at the slightest indication of your desire for me,
> I will make myself known to you.
> Watch for me at the very start of what you are about,
> not just when things get difficult or confusing.
> Be alert to me always
> and you will avoid a lot of trouble.
> You will find me, ever present, sitting at your
> conference tables and in your staff meetings.
> Just thinking about my presence will help you
> to develop a maturity of thought and understanding.
> Be aware of my presence, my concern, my willingness
> to inspire and to instruct you,
> and you will be amazed at how much you will decrease
> your own and everyone else's anxiety level.
> I journey with you and work through you,
> but also through and in those folks you come together with
> to be and to build church.
> As you meet with each other, I meet with each and all of you!

To believe that is to believe what Jesus promised: "For where two or three meet in my name, I shall be there with them." And to believe that, at the operational level, is to create and nurture a model of decision making that is truly church.

The shared wisdom model of church also calls us to make consistent efforts to incorporate prayer in the context of our meetings. But to be effective, group prayer must be well planned. Several suggestions for planning group prayer experiences are offered on pages 106-12 of Appendix I.

Focus Questions for Chapter 3

Answer the following questions to help you prepare for a discussion of them at your next meeting.

1. Reflect on your efforts to grow closer to your God.

What helps you grow closer to God? _____

_____

_____

What hinders? _____

_____

_____

2. What is your experience of—

living on automatic? _____

_____

_____

living your daily experience in prayer? _____

_____

_____

3. Consider your need to grow spiritually. What would be your—

prime time? _____

_____

_____

God space? _____

_____

_____

method? _____

_____

_____

4. Reflect on and discuss this statement: "It is not possible for me to hear the God of the Gathering if I am not in touch with the God of my lived experience."

_____

_____

4

The Problems

There is no model, method, or procedure for decision making that is guaranteed to work. Each model has its own problems inherent in its structure as well as the ones we create as we go about implementing the model. I prefer to think of these as concerns but must admit that sometimes they are problems. The three that I explore in this chapter are the ones that I have met most consistently as I have worked with the shared wisdom model: the idea that the shared wisdom model is a feminist approach to decision making, the question of the efficiency of the model, and the question of who discerns.

A FEMINIST APPROACH?

The issue of the role of women is a critical one both in church and in society. It is not my purpose to deal at length with this topic, although it is one close to my heart. But there are too many paradigmatic implications and ramifications for the shared wisdom model to ignore it.

In Paul I. Murphy's *La Popessa* he writes of Eugenio Cardinal Pacelli's dilemma at finding himself accepting the superior intelligence of Sister Pascalina:

> In one respect it was grating to Pacelli to seek such extraordinary advice from a nun. Here he was, the Vatican Secretary of State, long imbued with the prejudice of male supremacy and certain of his conviction that the hierarchy is all-knowing, having to bow to a woman's intellect. (1)

In one way, the best response to such an observation is laughter. The difficulty is, however, that it simply contains too much truth. And not just about the hierarchy and nuns. We could change the nouns and, as long as we retained the male-female identity, find ourselves with a painful and all too often accurate scenario played out in today's church.

I have worked with all manner of church groups, suggesting a possible problem with the parliamentary model and hinting that win-lose just might not be the appropriate frame of reference. I have even been so bold sometimes as to suggest that a more spiritual, intuitive approach might be what we are being called to—an approach that would include a willingness to let go, that is, to work without having to win. In all these cases it has typically been the women in the audience who have been able to hear what I was trying to say. It was certainly not exclusively women who understood, nor did all women understand. But I would say that for every man who seemed to be able to hear what I was trying to say, there would be at least three or four women who would be nodding and looking all too knowingly at me. And this occurred in audiences that were fairly evenly divided in terms of men and women present.

It has also been my experience that women religious have been doing the best job with the shared decision making process. They are the ones who have moved, often very gradually and sometimes without even naming the process, into a model that has the components of prayer, shared wisdom, letting go, and seeking consensus. These are the components of the model that I call a shared wisdom model.

There is obviously something in this model that matched the so-called feminine consciousness—something that women seem more comfortable with, seem more in tune with than do many men.

We need to consider some realities. Given the cultural expectations, training, and experience of what works for us, we have developed some typically masculine and feminine behaviors and attitudes. For example, competitiveness is recognized as a male quality. This is not to say that all men are competitive and women are not. But it is to say that a vast majority of men will, in fact, be very much at home with competition and a great number of women will find it distasteful.

The lists of so-called masculine and feminine qualities are endless, but they do have some commonality. This commonality comes out of the learned expectations put upon men and women as well as their lived experience of what has worked for them (or worked for their mothers or fathers). It seems safe to say, given the research and the experience, that a large percentage of men, when they put their heads in automatic and are most comfortable with how they think, feel, and act, will tend to be analytical, selective in their analysis, competitive, and controlling. A large percentage of women, on the other hand, when they put their heads in automatic and are most comfortable with how they think, feel, and act, will find themselves synthesizing information, taking a holistic approach, wanting to collaborate, and being quite sensitive to how all the above is happening or not happening.

Now, if we consider the two models of decision making that we have been discussing, we find certain characteristics associated with each one.

1. A parliamentary model tends to be—
   - analytical,
   - selective,
   - competitive,
   - controlling.

2. A shared wisdom model tends to be—
   - synthesizing,
   - holistic,
   - collaborative,
   - enabling.

Do you see the potential problem? For starters, we live, serve, and worship in a male-dominated church. Reflect with me just briefly on this reality as it is stated by Joan Ohanneson in her book *Woman: Survivor in the Church.*

> For centuries, the question has been asked and answered for her by others—primarily the wise and good and holy men in the church. They have described her, defined her, instructed her, legislated for her without ever once consulting her. ("What do you need? How do you feel? What do you think?") Apparently, they never thought her reality was important enough to warrant seeking her input. Her worth was seen in terms of whom those churchmen needed her *to be* (servant, laborer, domestic) *for them.* (2)

Then there are all the historical realities of the past twenty years of renewal. Not the least among these is the position taken by most councils and boards that they are about the "business part" of decision making in church. And who typically makes decisions in business? You guessed it!

This understanding of roles and responsibilities has all too often been strengthened by the consultation of well-meaning management firms and consultants who were brought in from the business world to assist boards and councils to understand their roles and develop their structures. This inevitably led to the strengthening of a masculine approach that rewarded competitiveness and the desire to win and to control.

It is not at all my desire to point a finger at any one person or group within church. It is a fact, however, that none of us, men or women, have been big into androgyny! So I come along with a model of church that looks feminine—at first glance not even androgynous, but out and out feminine! It frowns on needing to win; it wants to gather as much wisdom as possible in an obviously holistic approach; it leans toward synthesizing and finds collaboration much more effective than competition in its approach to arriving at a final decision. Such a model understandably frightens, threatens, confuses, or just isn't worth being taken seriously by those who work out of a male consciousness.

This is a very sensitive area and one that can easily lead to misunderstanding. It is critical to the proper understanding of the model that people realize I am not saying that only feminine qualities are necessary or desirable. That is not androgyny. Nor is it Christian feminism. There is a great difference between Christian feminism and radical feminism. Unfortunately, I believe, the latter is what makes the headlines and provides most of our understanding of the feminist movement. Radical feminism is just that—radical. It seeks to do away with anything masculine, to live life without the help of men, thank you. It is, in effect, the reverse of male chauvinism. Christian feminism seeks to incorporate and blend masculine and feminine qualities and gifts and to respect the equality that such a blending makes possible.

It is not just in church or in the Christian feminist movement that we find this move toward androgyny. Such a trend is becoming prominent in industry and management models as well. The so-called Japanese model has done much to bring this new approach to the attention of the industrialized nations. Particularly at the level of management is the intuitive, collaborative, sensitive, holistic approach being recognized as viable and valuable.

Matthew Fox deals with much of this at some length in his book *A Spirituality Named Compassion.* He shows two different approaches to being and building church, which he calls "climbing Jacob's ladder" and "dancing Sarah's circle." Speaking of our traditional dependence on the ladder system, he observes:

> Competition is built into ladder climbing. . . . On a ladder one
> studies one's competition and knows well exactly who is on the
> rung above and who is pushing from below. Competition and
> combat are intrinsic to ladder climbing. In contrast, circle dancing
> is not about competition at all but about sharing ecstasies. There
> is always room for another person in a circle and in fact the fun of
> all is increased, not threatened, by the arrival of a new dancer. . . .
> There are no winners and losers in such a schema—only dancers
> with the dance in common. . . . When one is climbing a ladder
> one's hands are occupied with one's precarious survival and can-

not be extended to assist others without putting one's climb and even one's life—if one is high enough up the ladder—in jeopardy. In contrast, when one dances a circular dance one's hands are freed to extend to others in assistance and in celebration. They are also freed to ask for and to receive assistance. (3)

After suggesting that Jesus' approach was far from ladder climbing and much more in tune with dancing Sarah's circle, Fox observes:

Churches today are dealing with the passage from climbing Jacob's ladder to the dancing of Sarah's circle. This movement is demonstrated, for example, in the emergence of team ministries . . . another example of church responding to Sarah's circle is the declaration of Vatican II that church means primarily the "people of God." To define church as people or as the folks is a far cry from defining it as hierarchy. It is Sarah's cry, not a cry from the ladder top. The implications of this radical statement by the bishops themselves are still being born and worked out. (4)

At the end of this chapter, Fox quotes a poem, "In Search of a Round Table," by Chuck Lathrop, a contemporary American poet currently living in Ireland. I, too, wish to quote from this poem because it has, I believe, much to say to us as we continue our pursuit of a shared wisdom model of church, a model that is not about climbing ladders. This is a model that must learn to dance Sarah's circle (not to be confused, by the way, with going around in circles!).

Concerning the why and how and what and who of ministry,
one image keeps surfacing;
A table that is round.

It will take some sawing
to be roundtabled,
some redefining
and redesigning

Such redoing and rebirthing
or narrowlong Churching
can painful be
for people and tables

But so was the cross,
a painful too table
of giving and yes

And from such death comes life,
from such dying comes rising,
in search of roundtabling
And what would roundtable Churching mean?

It would mean no daising and throning,
for but one King is there,

and He was a footwasher,
at table no less . . .

For at the narrowing tables,
servant and mirror
become picture framed
and centers of attention

And crosses become but gilded ornaments
on bare stone walls
in buildings used but once a week only

But the time and the tables
are changing and rearranging
And what of narrowlong tableministers,
when they confront
a roundtable people
after years of working up the table
(as in "up the ladder")
to finally sit at its head,
only to discover
that the table has turned around???

Continued rarified air
will only isolate
for there are no people there,
only roles

They must be loved into roundness,
where *apart* is spelled *a part*
and the call is to the gathering

For God has called a People,
not "them and us"

"Them and us"
are unable
to gather round,
for at a roundtable,
there are no sides

And ALL are invited
to wholeness and to food . . .
Roundtabling means
no preferred seating,
no first and last,
no better, and no corners
for "the least of these"

Roundtabling means
being with,
a part of
together, and one

It means
room for the Spirit
and gifts
and disturbing profound peace for all . . .

And it is we in the present
who are mixing and kneading
the dough for the future.

We can no longer prepare for the past . . . (5)

Allow me one last point on where we seem to be going as church in all of this. In her "A Feminine Critique of the Peace Pastoral" Sister Joan Chittister makes the point that this major document of the American bishops has, in fact, taken a feminist approach. She writes:

> . . . in a world designed by males whose theology has told them that to be male is to be a superior being, the feminine qualities of the human soul have often been both repressed and resisted as signs of weakness. . . . Masculine traits are in general more valued than feminine ones, even among women themselves. To choose to act out of feminine values in this society, then, would at least be charismatic, if not absurd. . . .

> But the foolish femininity of a Gospel centered on a cross is of the essence of the Christian dispensation. It is not of the essence of the political relations of the Christian world, however. In the document "The Challenge of Peace" the American bishops are clearly struggling between the two.

> . . . at significant moments, the choices between a masculine power paradigm and the feminine principle of peacemaking emerge in the document with prophetic clarity.

> . . . in significant ways the pastoral is basically feminist. It rejects control, aggression, competition and reason as ultimate values of human growth and calls by implication for flexibility, submissiveness, support, feeling, eros and self-sacrifice. It is precisely on those grounds that it is being criticized as "foolish," "incompetent," "weak," and even "ridiculous." Women have known the criticism for eons.

> At the same time, no document of the American Catholic church sounds more like the Gospel, unglossed, unwarped and undistorted. (6)

My point? As we have attempted during these years of renewal to develop collegial models of decision making, we have, in Fox's imagery, tried to dance Sarah's circle. But, for the most part, we've done it while still involved in ladder climbing!

The choice to follow a basically secular, parliamentary model has only served to enhance the masculine values of logic, control, competition, reason, a sense of order, and self-development. The shared wisdom model is more clearly related to Sarah's circle. It is about spontaneity, intuition, letting go, being in touch with feelings as well as with the intellect. It seeks to take that holistic approach that is generally defined as feminine.

Men and women alike have learned the ladder skills well. Now it is time for us to begin to define and own and practice the circle skills. The concern about the place of women in the church today is appropriate. Women have much to offer the church and much to offer the shared wisdom model.

I simply want to call women and men in church to be all that they can be. I want to encourage women to name this gift we call feminine consciousness, to treasure it in themselves, and to continue to offer it to church. I wish also to call women in church to support those men who are coming to recognize the feminine qualities as the gift they are. There are many such men in today's church—receptive, supportive men who are open to the call of the Spirit. Not only do these men recognize the gift women bring to church, but they also call other men to the same realization. It is out of this respectful understanding that the men in church will come to value the nourishing of these so-called feminine qualities in their own personalities. There are many men in today's church who have developed their own intuitive understandings and insights, men who have little need to be competitive and controlling. I have been singularly blessed to know and work with so many of them. They need the assurance that such a holistic development of their own potential is not a sign of masculine weakness but rather a sign of human strength! "Male and female He created them." Such was the wisdom of God! It becomes clearer and clearer just how much we need each other if we are to be true to our creation!

So now as we move on to the actual design of the model and the many practical implications, you may find your masculine consciousness rejecting, doubting, or fearing the model, or not even taking it or me seriously. I only ask that you read on, recognizing that the author is a woman whose own masculine consciousness has had to work through much of the same feelings and doubts. The result of the struggle for me has been a blending of the two, an androgyny of thought that, I believe, does reflect the call of the Gospel and the challenge to be and to build church.

BUT IS IT EFFICIENT?

As I have worked with various groups around the country, one of the major concerns about the shared wisdom model has been the question of efficiency. The questions go like this:

- Won't this approach take longer? (Yes!)
- Is it really an efficient way to solve problems and make decisions? (Not if by "efficiency" you mean can we get through an eleven-point agenda in two hours.)
- How can we be sure that we'll reach a discerned decision by the time we need an answer? (Only by good planning that leaves time for the Spirit. It is, in my experience, not possible to program the Spirit.)
- And what about all this talk about prayer? Increasing my own prayer life? Involving the group in prayerful reflection? I didn't join this council (board, team, staff) to pray. I joined it to be a decision maker! (Perhaps we had better take a serious look at *why* people become members of these groups and what the expectations are for the individual as well as the group.)

I do not mean to dismiss these concerns so lightly. In fact, as we move along I will devote a great deal of time to process and planning and certainly to the whole question of spirituality and prayer. These are all serious concerns. The model that I propose does ask more of its members both in terms of time commitment and personal holiness. The emphasis, remember, is on the being and building of church, not simply on an improved management model. It is not, however, an impossible approach. It resembles the call of the Spirit, so evident in today's church, to involve the laity, not just because of their skills and experience, but also out of their own personal response to deeper spirituality.

THE AVAILABILITY OF THE GIFT: Who Discerns?

So, who does discern? Who can be involved in a shared wisdom model? Is this model calling us to an elitist approach, to boards and councils in which only a select few can be considered for membership? Is it only those who are outstandingly holy, obviously prayerful, and known to demonstrate their Christianity beyond all doubt who will be involved in this model?

The discernment tradition would seem to lead in this direction. Much is said in that tradition about long experience, tested holiness, and much practice in the Christian life.

On the one hand, I do not want to ignore the tradition, nor do I want to belittle the importance of holiness as a prerequisite to being attentive to the Spirit. On the other hand, I'm back to my conviction that a gift of the Spirit can hardly be limited to a special few. Jesus did say:

> For where two or three meet in my name, I shall be there
> with them.   *Matthew 18:20*

> And know that I am with you always.   *Matthew 28:20*

> The Advocate, the Holy Spirit, whom the Father will send
> in my name, will teach you everything.   *John 14:26*

That hardly sounds elitist! It hardly sounds as though the gift of discernment is meant only for a select few in the Christian community.

The challenge is to balance this availability of the Spirit promised by Jesus with the wisdom of the tradition that came to recognize the importance of spiritual growth and commitment to that growth. And I think the key to doing that is to clarify our expectations.

Both those who call others to the model and those who respond must be keenly aware of what is involved, of what the commitment is about. And just what is it about? As I see it, a call to be involved in a shared wisdom model of church is a call to ministry and a call to holiness. To accept such a call is to commit oneself to the dynamic process of spiritual growth that I call being church, while at the same time committing oneself to the equally dynamic ministry of building church, of working with others to make decisions for the diocese, the parish, the school, the team, the faculty, or the community.

All too often, in the past, we have had little, no, or very strange criteria for membership on boards and councils. Our approach to people has frequently imaged this confusion. How many people have found themselves on nominating lists because someone said, "Father really needs a few more folks on the ballot," or "Come on, you can do it. After all it's only one meeting a month." At least these approaches are neutral. Far worse is the invitation that goes like this: "We've really had it with the lack of accountability for finances in this parish. You're a respected financier. We need you to get on that council and keep the pastor honest!"

The sad result of these scenarios and many related ones is that many well-intentioned and good people get on boards and councils without any real insight as to why they are there. Or, as in the case of the financier in my scenario, they come on with goodwill but for all the wrong reasons. Any board or council, or any member of a board or council, whose motivation is to "get" the pastor, the bishop, the principal, or to keep them honest, in line, or jumping, has most likely missed the most important point of being in this ministry. It is very difficult to reconcile the "get 'em" mentality with a call to ministry, a call to be and to build church. I am not at all opposed to accountability, and will address this issue when I speak about evaluation (pages 94–95, 144). But what we have in this negative approach is a mind-set, a mentality, a goal that guarantees an adversary position and relationship. That is not the climate in which ministry is most productive. It is precisely this negative climate or expectation that sets the stage for the fights, the power struggles, and the win-lose scenarios.

Now, add to this the all too often misunderstood concept of the nature and purpose of the group: that it is to be about the "business" of church. The generally accepted mentality in the business world assumes an adversary position. This is the frame of reference out of which labor-management relations are born. It is the competitive god that is called on to bless the so-called free enterprise system. It is closely related to what we have come to identify as the masculine approach to business, profits, and up-the-ladder success.

I submit that this approach is destructive of what we are attempting to build: church. I further submit that this is becoming more and more obvious to both leaders and members of various church decision-making groups. It is this growing understanding that has led so many people all over the country and at all levels of church to begin to look for new approaches to decision making. While still retaining the basic parliamentary model, they have made significant adjustments in such areas as criteria for membership, formation, and conduct of meetings.

But even given this growing awareness of the need to redesign or redirect decision-making groups, I still find so many people, especially pastors and others in leadership and staff positions, extremely hesitant to consider criteria for membership on boards and councils. They especially resist any suggestion that there might be limits placed on such membership. The general feeling is that if you are alive and well and breathing and willing, you are eligible. And the hope is that once you become a member, the board or council will be able to form or train you or do whatever is necessary. I submit that such an approach is lacking in wisdom and is not realistic. Nor is it true to the tradition of formation that is such a part of our Catholic heritage.

This attitude may well be related to our understanding of democracy and the great American dream that any kid on the block can grow up to be president, thus forcing us to allow anyone who happens along to take a crack at it!

Even though I find such hesitancy on the part of many to work through any criteria for membership, I have no difficulty getting these same leaders and staff members to readily agree that if boards and councils are really going to be part of the mission of church, the people on them must be able to see themselves as called to ministry. Now, think about that for a minute. Ministry is a calling, a vocation. One is moved by God's grace, touched by God's intervention in one's life, called to serve in a special way, to give of one's life or talents or time or all of the above.

Traditionally in the church, such a calling has been tested in a variety of ways. True, formation played a very significant role in the process of becoming a priest, a sister, a brother. But there was also much testing of the mind, the heart, the spirit of the person who expressed a desire to serve the Lord and the church. Both the individual who felt the call and the "authorities" who were in a position to accept that individual for ministry had to have ample proof that the call was from God.

I submit that we must build this concept into the criteria for the ministry of serving on boards and councils.

But we should be concerned with more than criteria. Our ministers—clergy, sisters, brothers—not only have made a commitment but have been trained and formed for what that commitment will ask of them as they live it out. Ministry demands formation. The minister must deal with the theology and psychology of ministering, learn some skills, practice these skills under supervision, and integrate all of this into a spirituality and a life-style. Only then is he or she ready to take on the lived experience of actually being a minister and growing with the experience. We call that training and formation by a variety of names. We say that the young man has gone to the seminary or that the young woman is in the novitiate or at the house of formation. It would just not occur to us to ask anyone to take up the responsibilities of priesthood, for example, without such a training program. The person accepting the call to priesthood needs the time, the space, and the place as well as the guidance to test the call and to learn how to respond to it.

In recent years we have begun to translate this expectation beyond the so-called professional religious. As more and more of the laity answer the call to full-time ministry in church as pastoral assistants, principals, religious education directors, and heads of diocesan departments and offices, the need not only for professional preparation but also for programs of formation is becoming more widely accepted. We also see this trend deepening in terms of lay faculty members in our schools. Most diocesan school offices have developed formation programs specifically to respond to this need.

Now, I believe it is time to translate these understandings of expectations, criteria, and formation to the arena of the decision makers in our parishes, dioceses, and educational ministries. Such an approach will not have the degree of sophistication that will be found in a seminary or a ministry training program for full-time professional ministry, but it will have the basic components.

If we are to look seriously at how a person responds to the call to be and to build church, I submit that we must develop programs and procedures that will include the following:

- Ways in which people can become alert to the possibility that they have a call to ministry
- A process to enable people to get in touch with their own giftedness
- Adequate information about the needs of the parish/diocese for ministry
- A process to enable people to match their giftedness to the needs expressed by the parish/diocese
- A process to enable people to discern the possibility of being called to ministry, specifically in this model
- Well-defined expectations with regard to both initial formation and training and ongoing formation and training

Suggestions for how all this can happen will be dealt with in Chapter 8. Let me clarify here, however, that I am not talking about membership on a board or a council being limited to people who think alike! That would destroy one of the most important concepts of the shared wisdom philosophy: that we all have different pieces of the wisdom and that we acquire the total wisdom the Spirit wishes to share with us only as we gather those different pieces. Nor am I saying that only extremely pious, highly skilled, and perfectly motivated folks are eligible for election to boards and councils. What I am trying to say is that the criteria for membership on boards and councils must include the following:

- A willingness to recognize this call as a call to holiness and, out of this recognition, to commit one's energies to the process of growing in holiness
- A willingness to see this call as a call to ministry and therefore to accept formation and training both in preparation for membership and as an expected part of the experience of being a board or council member

It is this kind of willingness that I believe can be translated as the tested holiness that comes out of the tradition. People's willingness to embark on this ministerial journey and their understanding of what the journey is about will open them to the Spirit who will journey with them and speak through them. They will learn to be responsive both to the God of their lived experience and to the God of the Gathering. They will be available to the Spirit so that through them and in them the wisdom of the Spirit will be seen and heard. And in this process of becoming more spiritually alive, that is, of being church, they will be able to build church, that is, to minister!

Focus Questions for Chapter 4

1. Reflect on the way you make decisions and solve problems.

Do you tend to be analytical, selective, competitive, and controlling? Or are you more likely to be synthesizing, holistic, collaborative, and enabling?

What does this tell you about the development of your so-called masculine and feminine qualities?

What connection does this understanding of yourself have with your willingness to consider a shared wisdom model?

2. Consider this statement: "Women have much to offer the church and much to offer this model."

How do you feel about this statement? _____

What do you think women have to offer? _____

3. Recall your own motives and expectations as you became a member of this group.

How was it (or was it?) a call to ministry? _____

How do you feel about committing yourself to a group that is about more than just the "business" of church?

4. What are the implications of these questions for your group as it now understands its roles and responsibilities?

5

The Process of Sharing Wisdom

What I have come to call the philosophy of shared wisdom is not the same as, but is built upon, the tradition of discernment, which was briefly discussed on pages 15-17. I believe this philosophy provides a way to translate that gift of the Spirit and make it available to the church today in the broad setting of shared decision making. I also believe that by taking the essence of the tradition and remolding it, it is possible to make both the experience and the process of sharing wisdom available to ordinary Catholics—lay, religious, or clerical, who know themselves to be called to holiness but are far from the hermit and cloistered religious.

These are the people who struggle with the frustrations they encounter on councils and boards. They are good people who reject the power plays, the infighting that is all too common to our present experience, but who still believe themselves to be called to involvement, responsibility, and commitment. It is for them (and I am one of them) that I attempt to develop this new model.

ATTITUDINAL REQUIREMENTS

Let us first look at the parts of the tradition that it would seem must be kept if the experience and the process are to be recognizable as the gift of discernment given the church by the Spirit. They are:

1. The sincere desire of those involved to grow in holiness so as to allow the voice of the Spirit to be heard in their lives and in their hearts

2. The ability to "let go," the "holy indifference" referred to in the tradition (see page 17), so as to be able to surrender to the voice of the Spirit when it is heard

3. The inclusion of prayer and solitude in the process, both as preparation for and as integral to the doing of discernment

4. The guidance of a spiritual leader or pastor to shepherd the discerners through the process

5. The sharing of all that the Spirit has revealed to each member of the group

6. The agreement among the members of the group either to work until consensus is reached or to agree with the majority decision

The reshaping of the tradition will need to include the following differences:

1. The discerners are not committed to a life of desert or cloistered asceticism. They are Christians of goodwill who seek to live in such a way that they are sensitive to the call and the touch of the Spirit in their own lived experience and in the God of the Gathering. They must develop a spirituality that fosters such sensitivity in the context of their lives.

2. What is to be discerned is not limited to decisions about one's personal spiritual life or even, strictly speaking, about the spirituality of the group. There will, in fact, be more so-called "secular" areas of concern than those we usually call "spiritual." A criterion needs to be developed so that groups can determine which issues really call for discernment.

3. The spiritual leader does not need to walk life's journey with the same degree of intensity and intimacy that the spiritual director of the tradition does. The role of this spiritual leader needs to be defined so that both leader and those led share common expectations.

4. Meetings should not be expected to go on forever, but prayer and solitude are absolutely necessary ingredients of every meeting. Preparation time in advance of each meeting needs to be designed and expected. The meetings need to be so organized that there is time for the reflective silence that enables the Spirit to be heard.

5. Responsibility for group process must be shared by all members, and the role of the leader must be designed so that he or she is clearly an enabler of people and a facilitator of process.

6. A new understanding of majority vote will need to be developed and internalized. It can no longer be the common understanding that the majority has won. Rather, it must reflect the Ignatian insight of the common understanding that the Spirit has been made manifest in the majority and therefore all must accept the decision of that majority as the discerned decision that all now agree to embrace.

PRACTICAL IMPLICATIONS

Let us now turn to the practical implications that are called for if the tradition is to come alive, if this gift of the Spirit is to be ours!

Any group that is planning to make use of this model of decision making will need to become familiar with the steps involved. There are three basic components:

1. Gathering the data
2. Reflecting prayerfully on the data
3. Sharing the wisdom that results from the reflection

These steps are repeated over and over again, as needed, until the group arrives at a decision that can be accepted gracefully by all the members of the group. This may be a consensus decision or a majority decision that all have agreed to accept as the call of the Spirit.

If the group has more than twenty-five members, it is likely that much of the discerning activity will go on at the committee, commission, or task force level rather than within the large group. At least much of the early process will take place in the smaller groups. Any discerned decision, however, must eventually be the work of the total group in that it is the total group who will come to recognize and accept the call of the Spirit.

Let us then examine the three steps and see what is involved in each one.

1. Gathering the data. This can be the most time consuming of all the steps. It involves gathering information from the "professionals" and from those to be affected by the possible decision. (Rule of thumb: Those to be affected by your decision have the right to share their wisdom with you *before* you make the decision.)

2. Reflecting prayerfully on the data. This is where analysis and synthesis take place *in each person's understanding* of the data. This step involves the effort of each member of the group to reflect on the data in terms of his or her lived experience and insights and to listen to the promptings of the Spirit in the depths of the heart.

3. Sharing the wisdom. Having reflected prayerfully and touched one's own wisdom, each member must now share that wisdom with the total group and listen to all the other members as they share their wisdom. This is where analysis and synthesis take place *in the group thinking.* The effort here is again to try to hear the wisdom of the Spirit coming through the wisdom being shared within the group.

When the wisdom is shared, it becomes new data which then needs to be identified, clarified, and nuanced so that the group can reflect on it and then share that reflection. Thus the cycle often needs to be repeated, perhaps many times, before any decision will be made.

Data Collection

The process for making a discerned decision, then, starts with the collection of data. Before starting this process the group must agree on just how much data is needed. Many people find it impossible to discern a decision because they do not have enough information available to them. The reverse problem can also exist. I've seen groups become so involved in collecting sufficient data that they never arrive at the decision-making point in the process. To determine the amount of data to be gathered the group must simply agree on how much information is really needed. The amount of professional data required would typically be left to the professionals involved to determine. Input from others can be determined by asking, "Who will be affected by this decision?" and then following the rule of thumb: Those to be affected have the right to share their wisdom with you *before* you make the decision. This does not mean that you must always hear from all those to be affected. Often a representative or random group will prove to be sufficient. If, for example, you are dealing with a major shift in liturgical policy, the question to ask is whether you need to seek the opinions of all parishioners or if a random sampling will give you basically the same data. Another rule of thumb might be helpful here: If faced with a choice between "too much" or "not enough" input, I would suggest that you choose the "too much" option.

There is also the possibility that a random sampling would give you adequate data but that the people not asked would be less than happy with the fact that their wisdom was not solicited. The decision to survey the total parish might be a sensitive response to the desire of many parishioners to be involved in the life of the parish. All of these possibilities need to be discussed and weighed before the group collecting the data decides how to accomplish this task.

This stage of data gathering is vitally important to the total process and needs to be done by people who have certain skills and are willing to give the kind of time commitment required to do an adequate job. In addition to organizational skills, listening skills are critical to this task. While the temptation here is to split the work up among many people, it is my experience that data collection is often done best by a relatively small task force that has more staff people on it than board or council members. Whoever does it and however it is done, if discernment is to be valid, adequate data must be gathered.

The success of this first step of the process will depend not only on how adequate the information is but also on how well the sources of information are identified and how clearly the data is reported back to the discerning group. Simplicity is always the key to success and a great rule to follow.

Reflection on the Data

When all necessary data has been gathered, it is given to the decision-making group for prayerful reflection, the second step of the process. The effort here is to study and reflect on the data in terms of one's own lived experience, praying through feelings, insights, knowledge, and reactions. Out of this prayerful reflection comes each member's "piece of the wisdom" to be shared with the total group. Keep in mind the importance of scheduling sufficient time between the dissemination of the data and the meeting in which the wisdom is to be shared. Some people will need many days for reflective thought. Depending on how long and involved the report is, lead time for reflection can vary from five or six days to two weeks or even longer. Again, all of this must be thought through in advance so that a realistic timetable can be planned.

Sharing the Wisdom

Now the third step, sharing the wisdom, can take place. There are several ways to design this step. At times, for example, the group may want to deal with the negatives first. Negative attitudes are often generated by fear, misinformation, or simply a lack of information. By dealing with such items first the discerners are able to free their hearts and heads from such negative and binding realities. Once the fears are owned and the information is checked for accuracy, the discerners are ready to move on to the positive concepts, which would allow for greater attentiveness to the Spirit. At other times such an approach just does not match the subject or the needs of the group. What is always critical at this point in the process is the honesty of sharing, the openness to hearing one another, and the fostering of that "letting go" attitude. Efforts must be made to listen for trends, similar pieces of wisdom coming from different members, and, equally important, unique concepts and different approaches to the wisdom.

After discussing the wisdom that has been shared, a synthesis is made either by the group leader or by the facilitator working with the group (if there is one). This synthesis then becomes the new data and the group is asked to move back into prayerful reflection. The amount of time needed for this will depend on the amount of data and its complexity. Oftentimes it is clear that there is so much to be sifted through that it cannot be done in a limited period of time. If this is the case, the best approach is to leave the process and plan a time to return to it, possibly at the next scheduled meeting. It is wise to check such a decision with the group members and allow them to decide how much time they need, taking into consideration that a certain amount of compromise may be required.

It is at this point in the discernment that the time factor often becomes the tail that wags the dog! If people get nervous about the need for a decision, they will tend to truncate the process. This almost always leads to a decision that can hardly be called discerned. There may be a situation that calls for an immediate answer or solution. That's life! But then the group should recognize that and simply agree not to go for discernment but to be satisfied with a majority vote that may or may not be accepted by the minority but will at least provide the temporary decision that is needed. Such a decision might well be brought before the group at a later date for a discerned decision that would be more lasting.

The key here, of course, is good planning. There will be emergencies, but most decisions that will come before a board or a council, a staff or a team, can be foreseen. An important part of annual goal setting is the identification of such areas and issues a year in advance so that meetings can be scheduled and planned accordingly. Groups that consistently find themselves faced with decisions that should have been made yesterday are usually lacking in good planning and goal-setting procedures.

We are now in the second round of sharing wisdom. From this, more new data may well result, calling for additional reflection. And so it continues until the facilitator or leader of the group recognizes the beginning of a consensus. The indicator of this is that more and more people are beginning to come to the same conclusions. At this point a consensus test is appropriate. The clearest way to test the degree of consensus is just to ask the question: "If you were to vote on this issue now, given the ideas and feelings you have all heard from one another and matching that wisdom to your own, how would you vote?" This is not the time for debate or even for explanations of why a person votes one way or another. Just a simple yes or no is all that is required.

Sometimes, wondrously, the very first consensus test reveals that a consensus has been reached! Usually it indicates a future direction. Sometimes it just highlights the wide variety of ideas and directions that are still present in the group. Unless there is, in fact, a consensus, the testing procedure provides new data which then must be discussed and addressed first in the group. Questions like "Can those of you who 'voted' against the issue help the rest of us understand your reasons?" are very helpful. After sufficient discussion the group is now ready to move back into prayerful reflection and the cycle continues to repeat itself for as long as is necessary.

It will sometimes happen that the group realizes it does not have sufficient information to continue the discernment. For example, let us say that a liturgy team was attempting to discern the possibility of renovating the sanctuary. Its responsibility would be to eventually arrive at a position and a recommendation that could be presented to the parish council for their discernment. As the liturgy committee moves through the various stages of the process, they may come to realize that the financial figures they are dealing with are more guesswork than they are real estimates. There is no way the parish council can continue the discernment without some accurate cost estimates. At this point, then, the process is temporarily discontinued and the additional data is gathered and then presented to the liturgy team for its reflection and discussion. Then the process continues.

Keep in mind that the ultimate goal in all of this is to let the discerning group arrive at a decision with which every member of the group will be able to live gracefully. So as the process continues there must be a balance of the "letting go" attitude with the willingness on the part of each member to speak his or her wisdom. Also, each person must make an effort to listen carefully and respectfully to every other person. A rule of thumb is worth noting: If my piece of the wisdom matches at least one other person's, it is probably important to keep bringing it up for consideration. If, on the other hand, after multiple rounds of the process, I am the only one taking a specific position, chances are that it is time to let go and attempt to listen more attentively to the wisdom of the group.

SPIRITUAL LEADERSHIP

There is another significant consideration that needs to be explored: the role of the spiritual leader or pastor during this process. Chapter 6 is devoted to the place of spiritual leadership in a discerning model, but I need to say something here about that very important role.

The issue here is whether the leader plays a different role than the other members of the group. For example, does he or she come to the group with the answer already in place? Is the leader the prophet who calls the group to a prediscerned decision? Or is the leader as much a part of the discernment as other members of the group?

As I understand the tradition, the leader is called to be with the group in the search. The spiritual leader—be that the bishop, pastor, superior, principal, vicar—is called to be "prophet" only in the sense of calling the members of the group to purity of heart that they might pray for light. In this sense the leader assists them in their efforts to get in touch with their own religious experience by faith sharing, and calls them to search in their own hearts for the will of God and the strength and courage to speak that will and to follow it as it emerges in the process. But all the while the leader is to be equally involved in the struggle, the questions, the faith sharing, the willingness to "let go" and to follow the guidance of the God of the Gathering!

RELATIONSHIP OF COMMITTEES TO THE TOTAL GROUP

If the initial discerning has been done by a committee or task force or commission, that group will need to prepare its report and recommendations for presentation to the larger group. The smaller group should share as much data as seems necessary and helpful, keeping in mind that all its work should not be repeated by the entire board or council or staff. However, the stages that the discernment went through and the rationale for the final decisions will need to be explained in some detail.

At this point the larger group will have all the data it needs to move into prayerful reflection. It will then share the fruits of the reflection which, very often, is to accept the smaller group's recommendations. This is most apt to happen (1) when the trust level in both groups is high and (2) when the report from the smaller group is thorough and complete.

However, if immediate agreement is not forthcoming, two options are possible. The larger group may decide to repeat the discerning steps, that is, to deal with the data, reflect again, share the wisdom, and then continue these steps as often as is necessary to arrive at a decision. Or, it may decide to return the task to the smaller group and ask it to consider the new data generated by this hesitancy to approve, and to continue the discernment in the smaller group.

NEED FOR A FACILITATOR

One thing is very clear: Most groups using this process for the first time will need the assistance of an outside facilitator. How long will this need continue to be necessary? It really depends on the group and also on the issue. Some groups will have their own leadership potential to facilitate discernment. Often the spiritual leader will be able to function in this capacity, provided, of course, that he or she has genuinely learned the importance of that "letting go" stance. Even in those situations where such leadership is readily available within the group, some issues just do not lend themselves to internal facilitation. Often the issue will clearly call for someone who has absolutely no vested interest in the outcome. Such "hot issues" will be obvious as they arise. A few I can think of that I have facilitated include such things as the renovation of a motherhouse chapel, the possible closing of a parish school, the redesigning of diocesan structures, and the hiring of a principal. Before embarking on a discerning venture, the group must seriously consider what kind of leadership and/or facilitating it will need. I think I can guarantee that any group will need help at least until the members become familiar and comfortable with the process.

Evaluation of each attempt at a discerned decision will also be helpful and will provide an opportunity for the group to grow in its ability to use the model effectively. One of the tasks of the facilitator would be to lead the group in this kind of evaluation. Such an evaluation does not need to be lengthy but it must involve each member of the group. The facilitator would ask two questions: What was helpful/useful/good about the way the group arrived at this decision? What was not helpful/useful/comfortable about this process? All members would be encouraged to respond to each question. A brief discussion of these questions would enhance the process and would improve the members' participation in it the next time it is used.

Key to any group's openness to the Spirit through the process of discernment will be the willingness of each member in the group to accept and to surrender to the results of an evaluation.

ATTENTIVENESS TO THE SPIRIT

For a group to be about communal discernment, each member of the group must be walking with God, that is, committed to an openness to God, a trusting relationship that enables him or her to accept God's providence. The members of the group must also share some commonality in understanding and affirming the goal or mission of the group. And, finally, each member must exhibit a trust and an honesty both in the preparation stage and in the sharing of the wisdom.

As listening to the Spirit in one's own heart and head is key to the preparation stage, so, too, is listening key to the conversation stage. This is that time in the process of discernment when the pieces of the wisdom are gathered *by* the group *from* the group. The same criteria that are so central to the shared wisdom model—that is, sharing wisdom, hearing and treasuring wisdom, and creating a climate where these things can really happen—are found in the conversation stage.

There remains one other important learning to be applied to the shared wisdom model. All too often we have thought that if the group did not arrive at a consensus decision, discernment had not really happened. The tradition tells us that this is not necessarily so. The first clear account we have of the use of discernment for a group decision comes to us from Saint Ignatius and his little group of followers. They had to decide if they were going to become an "order" in the church or simply remain just a gathering of men trying to serve the church without any specific structural connection to it. One of the important things they agreed upon as they began their discerning process was that all "with one mind" would embrace the conclusions reached by a majority. It is a matter of history that these men did, in fact, reach a consensus, but it was not their primary aim.

Jules Toner, who has devoted a great deal of study and writing to this topic, explains:

> To conclude the reasoning together, it was their intention that all "with one mind" would embrace the conclusions reached by a majority vote. There are a number of things packed into this brief statement. They can be drawn out if we ask: How can they embrace with one mind a conclusion on which they have a split vote?
>
> First, they were ready to accept a conclusion by a simple majority vote, to accept it as that to which God in his infinite goodness had led them as "what the Holy Spirit had inspired." They did not expect unanimity nor demand it as necessary in order to trust their discernment and bring it to a satisfactory conclusion.
>
> Rather, they intended that unanimity would *follow* on the majority vote: all would embrace with one mind the conclusion recommended by a majority vote. Now, to have unanimity is not merely to have volitional consent of the intellectually dissenting minority to do what the majority wants. To have unanimity, the minority must cease to be an intellectually dissenting but volitionally consenting minority; that must now give *assent* to the majority conclusion as truly expressing the will of God. They must believe it is truly the right way, not merely the way which is legitimate because of a practical agreement to abide by the majority vote. (1)

This is a critical insight. It is also an insight that seems to have great difficulty penetrating our democratic notion of majority vote. Our experience tells us that to vote with the minority is to lose. The magnanimous loser is the one who, nevertheless, goes along with the majority and supports or at least does not block the action that flows from the decision. We call this being a good loser.

True discernment, however, cannot be about winning or losing. So how are we to reconcile a majority vote with an effort to discern? Obviously, a consensus decision is easier to recognize as the call of the Spirit to the group. But it is not a necessary outcome.

The discerning group must agree in advance that they will all be willing to accept the vote of the majority as the will of the Spirit. Let me say it another way: The minority must agree to agree with the majority even though their insights were not the same! Instead of an attitude of "we will do it this way because the majority want it this way," there will prevail an attitude of "we will do it this way because the Spirit has been heard through the majority." It is a faith response! And it is made possible by that holy indifference that must be nourished in each discerner.

There will sometimes be a member of the group who simply cannot surrender to the wisdom of the group, cannot believe the voice of God is to be heard in the group decision. Such a person does not experience the peace and contentment and joy that is clearly the experience of the others.

It is important to recognize the pain and/or the fear that is operating in such an individual. In no way are we to judge unkindly, to ridicule, or to become impatient with this person. Nor can we allow him or her to keep us from the will of the Spirit as discerned by the group. The group must move on while providing whatever loving support and healing seems appropriate or possible.

Please do not misunderstand what I am trying to say. A general feeling of contentment and peace, that ability to accept the decision gracefully, is, indeed, the indicator of a discerned decision. My only point is that it will not always be a unanimous experience, and I think that is acceptable and not something that should cause us to question the validity of the discernment.

Let us consider a situation in which there has been only a simple or a two-thirds majority. Before that can be declared a discerned decision it needs to be tested in some way. There must be a way of getting a reading from the group on the degree of contentment present. General discontent will lead us to recognize that we have not discerned the will of the Spirit.

I have found two very workable ways to do this, the choice of which depends on the nature of the decision to be made. When the group is seeking to discern a position to be taken on an issue or an action to be decided upon, I test the degree of consensus at any point in the process by asking, "The direction you are headed is gaining clarity. Is there anyone who cannot live with that direction?" In the early stages of the conversation this question tends to highlight differences, nuance concerns, and generally enrich the sharing of wisdom. It also provides new insights for prayerful consideration and reflection.

But as the process continues and it seems to be evident that the group is now going to reach at least a near consensus, I repeat my question, which becomes, for me, the barometer of when, in fact, the voice of the Spirit has been heard and accepted. General discontent on the part of the minority, a feeling that they cannot live with the decision of the majority, will send us back to the process for additional rounds of reflective prayer and wisdom sharing.

When the group is seeking the discernment of group leadership—a major superior or prioress of a community, a chairperson for a board or council, an administrator for a school or department—there is a different way to test the presence of the Lord's will. Allow me to use an example.

The setting was a parish council of twenty members. In a three-hour process the group had gone from identifying qualities they felt were needed for leadership to naming specific members on the council who had some of those qualities. The council finally agreed on three candidates. After a number of attempts to agree on a candidate, it became clear that one of the three was no longer in the running but that the group was "locked" into a nine-to-eleven vote on the other two. It was time for the test. I asked that every member of the council approach the candidate with the eleven votes (I'll call her Sally) and tell her if they would be able to accept her leadership and see her as the person designated by the Spirit to be their leader. Before doing that, however, each person was asked to spend fifteen minutes in prayerful reflection. During that time Sally and I prayed together and I explained to her that it was now her responsibility to "discern the discernment." She was to listen for a sense of more than acceptance of her personally, and to "read" the group in terms of contentment and peace. She was to ask herself if the group could accept her leadership gracefully.

At the end of those personal encounters, I asked Sally if she would accept the leadership of the council. Her answer was negative and her reason was clear. She explained that there were four members of the group who just could not gracefully accept her leadership. She rightfully saw this as an indicator that a decision had not been discerned.

So, humbly but honestly, we went back to the process. Because the meeting was already running long, the immediate past president of the council agreed to retain his position for another month at least, and another date was scheduled to continue the discernment. In the end, the candidate who was initially dropped was the one who finally became the chairperson. And the result was a peaceful and joyful acceptance by all members of the council.

There is nothing magical or miraculous about communal discernment! First of all, it is hard work. It takes all we have to give it, intellectually, emotionally, spiritually, and even physically in terms of endurance. It calls for a great amount of humility and simplicity of heart, a willingness to struggle with oneself and with one another, and, perhaps most importantly, a willingness to grow on the part of everyone involved.

Focus Questions for Chapter 5

1. Reflect on the three steps of the process: gathering the data, reflecting prayerfully, sharing wisdom.

   What is clear and makes sense to you?_____

   _____

   _____

   What is unclear? _____

   _____

   _____

2. Reflect on your understanding of the process at this point.

   What are the implications for you personally? _____

   _____

   _____

   What are the implications for the group? _____

   _____

   _____

   What are your hopes?_____

   _____

   _____

   What are your fears? _____

   _____

   _____

3. Reflect on and discuss why spirituality is such an important component of this model.

   _____

   _____

   _____

   _____

N.B.: Additional information on the use of discernment in group decisions can be found in Appendix II (pages 155-62). It might be helpful to read that material at this point in your study of the shared wisdom model.

Spiritual Leadership

As members of boards, councils, and senates, living out our baptismal commitment, we must be committed to transformation in our own lives, that is, to growing in our knowledge of and love for our God. We must open ourselves to the challenge to seek the wisdom of God in our own lived experiences and in the God of the Gathering. And we must be willing to accept help, to accept a guide, in this process.

In the tradition, the guide was called a spiritual director, a term not foreign to us today. Many of us have rediscovered the value of such a person in our lives. The spiritual director is one who walks the spiritual journey with us—one who listens, questions, affirms, challenges, and calls. Such a companion is essential to the discernment tradition and process. It is, therefore, important to translate the role of spiritual director to that of pastoral or religious or spiritual leadership if the shared wisdom model is to be true to that tradition.

Typically, at least at the parish and the diocesan levels, this person will be a priest—the pastor, the bishop, the vicar. While I am aware that there are other structures and situations in which this "pastoral" leadership is carried out by the nonordained—for example, religious superiors, principals, pastoral ministers, and so on—I choose to direct this section to the ordained minister. Those who do not find themselves in that category but are, indeed, pastoral leaders will have to make the necessary adaptations. I will, however, refer to this role as one of "spiritual leader" to give it more flexibility in our changing church structures.

In the experience of spiritual direction there is to be found an interesting and enriching dialectic. Both director and directee are touched deeply. While honesty and humility are called for on the part of the directee, there is the demand for openness, transparency, and vulnerability on the part of the director. While the latter may be in many ways the expert, the one more experienced, more advanced along the journey, the former is often used by the Spirit in wondrous ways in the life of the director. How often my own spiritual director has thanked me for the richness and insight that I have brought into his life. And I, in turn, have said much the same to the folks who come to me for direction.

This same dialectic will be operational in the relationship between the spiritual leader and the members of the board or council or staff. They will gift each other, and that ability to gift will flow from the mutual respect they develop and nourish toward one another.

This understanding is closely related to the concept, so important to this model, that no one has all the wisdom! Once we are genuinely convinced of that, we will be open to the word and guidance of the Spirit, whatever the source.

How will this direction, this nourishing of the spiritual wisdom, take place? It's primarily a matter of honest, open, and ongoing communication between spiritual leader and people. "When in doubt, have the conversation" has become my favorite rule of thumb! Ask the questions, explore the possibilities, share the lived experiences.

Let us consider this call of the spiritual leader to shepherd, gently guide, and honestly direct the members of the board or council. The challenge, the ministry, is to enable others to be and to build church.

For a wide variety of reasons, this call, this challenge, is often a painful one. This is especially true for members of the clergy whose image of leadership may be quite different from that of the enabling minister and whose role models have for the most part ministered in a pre-Vatican II church.

John Carroll Futrell clarifies the enormity of this shift when, in his article "Learning Leadership from Watershed Down," he compares the authoritarian leadership style, common before Vatican II, with the participative style of religious leadership called for by the Council. The authoritarian leader tended to be insulated or protected by "subordinate superiors." Often such a leader did not listen to community members and as a result offered solutions that did not fit the problems. The participative or enabling leader, on the other hand, is called to know the individuals, recognize their gifts as well as their limitations, animate the group to participation in discernment, and intuit the direction to which God is calling the community. Commenting on the centrality of leadership style, Futrell writes:

> . . . the quality of life of a community will be determined
> largely by the quality of its leadership. (1)

This theology of enabling ministry flows from the Council documents, and although I have already quoted *Lumen Gentium,* 37, it
bears repeating:

> The pastors, indeed, should recognize and promote the dig-
> nity and responsibility of the laity of the church. They should will-
> ingly use their prudent advice and confidently assign duties to
> them in the service of the church, leaving them freedom and
> scope for acting. Indeed, they should give them the courage to
> undertake works on their own initiative. They should with paternal
> love consider attentively in Christ initial moves, suggestions and
> desires proposed by the laity. Moreover, the pastors must respect
> and recognize the liberty which belongs to all in the terrestrial city.
> Many benefits for the church are to be expected from this
> familiar relationship between the laity and the pastors. The sense
> of their own responsibility is strengthened in the laity, their zeal is
> encouraged, they are more ready to unite their energies to the
> work of their pastors. The latter, helped by the experience of the
> laity, are in a position to judge more clearly and more appropriately
> in spiritual as well as in temporal matters. Strengthened by all her
> members, the church can thus more effectively fulfill her mission
> for the life of the world.

Bishop Carroll Dozier, speaking to *Lumen Gentium,* observes in
his article "The Bishop and the Community of the Local Church":

> . . . instead of placing the pope and the bishops at the top of
> the pyramid the church is pictured as a vast people on pilgrimage
> to the Father. People then become the center of the church of
> Jesus Christ, not its servants. This is a new concept which has
> taken us some time to assimilate.
> The more we consider the people of God as the basis of the
> church and as the church itself, the more we see that we are a
> group of pilgrims on our way to the Father and the more we begin
> to understand that we are called to be companions of Jesus Christ,
> as he is our companion. On the pilgrimage the ministries, various
> though they may be, play an important part in serving the needs of
> the pilgrims. (2)

This call to a new way of pastoring, obviously no small challenge,
is affirmed in the revised Code of Canon Law. In the Canon Law
Society's study for the parish ministry there is a section appropriately
entitled "Enabling Ministry." Reflecting on Canon 536, the author,
Bertram F. Griffin, a canon lawyer from Portland, Oregon, says:

> Pastors should be expected to develop among the laity a
> sense of shared responsibility and planning for the pastoral action
> and mission of the parish through the parish council. . . . Hence,

[pastors and future pastors] should be trained to have a sense of, and the necessary skills to develop shared responsibility, both in government and in ministry on the parish level. The pastor is involved in the life of his parishioners. This, however, does not mean that the pastor hugs ministry and decision making to himself, but, precisely because of his intimate involvement in the lives of so many people, he must enable them to take responsibility for the mission and direction of the church through the many ministries of the local church, both regarding the church's outreach mission to the world and the church's ministry to its own members. (3)

While the understanding of the Council documents places a new emphasis on the role of the laity, it certainly does not preclude the importance of pastoral leadership and shepherding. In his article Dozier comments that "the local bishop [translate: local pastor] shepherds his people in enabling them to serve one another."

Yet, it is not uncommon in my experience to have pastors viewing their position in the renewing church with a great deal of confusion and even frustration. Pastors have often told me that they feel they are no longer needed or that they do not have a clear role in the parish structure anymore. Some of them will just say, "I really don't know what it means to be a pastor in today's church."

This feeling of being unnecessary, or at least of questioning the role and its effectiveness, can lead to all manner of crippling behaviors and reactions. Yet, speaking out of his years of work as staff director to the Committee on the Parish of NCCB, Philip Murnion wrote in *America:*

When all is said and done, the pastor is the most crucial person in the parish. Almost unfailingly, we have found that where a parish enjoys vitality, the leadership of the pastor has been central to this vitality. On the contrary, where there are problems, the pastor's part in these problems is significant.

. . . We find there are many styles of good pastoring. Some good pastors are good teachers, some are good liturgists. Some have good organizational abilities, while others are remarkable for their one-to-one care. Still others are strong community builders, while others have a knack for hospitality that supports the efforts and the leadership of others.

There is no one style of good pastoring, yet there are some common qualities. Good pastors seem to have a confident sense of direction. Aware of their own abilities and of their own weaknesses, they have a good notion of what a parish can be. Second, good pastors care about their people. They show respect for the experience and abilities of people and are as ready to listen as to speak. They listen carefully and really hear what people are saying. Third, good pastors are able to share decision making and leadership. Their strength evokes the strength of others. Weak pastors evoke the weaknesses of others, their tendency to dependency, pettiness or divisiveness. Fourth, good pastors seem to be interested in both the developments in theology and the life of the larger church beyond their parishes. (4)

My point? If the shared wisdom model is to work, we need good pastoring, good church leadership. We need a shepherd who can provide direction while at the same time recognizing that he too is a pilgrim who walks the journey not always ahead of his people but sometimes with, and now and then even behind, them.

The spiritual leader, especially if he is a pastor, must achieve a balance between his responsibility to doctrine, policy, authority, and so on, and his responsibility to enable and free people to develop their gifts and take their rightful place in the mission of the church. Such a balance is not easy to define, much less to live out. The centrality of the role of leader cannot be overemphasized. It was not without intent that Jesus, in his efforts to model leadership, called Himself the Good Shepherd!

In the shared wisdom model the spiritual leader is, first and foremost, called to a sensitivity of the presence of the Spirit both in the group and in the leader's own lived experience. The importance of processing life (see Chapter 3, pages 21-23)—of daily asking the question, "What's it all about, Alfie?"—is the frame of reference within which the leader feels comfortable with the role. Saint Augustine offers a helpful reflection as quoted in *Lumen Gentium,* 32:

> When I am frightened by what I am to you, then I am consoled by what I am with you. To you I am the bishop, with you I am a Christian. The first is an office, the second a grace; the first a danger, the second salvation.

As leader, it is out of the pastor's acceptance of his dual role as "leader-member of the community" that he is able to trust himself and his insights and sensitivity to the Spirit in the group. This is what will make it possible for him to recognize and name any lack of sensitivity to the Spirit when such is exhibited by the group. When the group is headed for a win-lose confrontation, he must not only be aware of the dynamic but name it and call the members back to the "let go" approach they have committed themselves to. When the group does not seem to be listening to the wisdom of the Spirit in one another, or, perhaps, even in themselves, it is he who must call them to quiet, prayerful reflection. As spiritual leader, no matter what the agenda or how heated the topic, no matter how "secular" the issue, he has the responsibility of keeping the members of the group true to their commitment to be about church! This is what we are talking about when we say that the spiritual leader is to walk the journey with the group, which makes his role not unlike that of the spiritual director in the tradition.

However, as pastor, the spiritual leader also has another responsibility, that ultimate responsibility for affirming the discerned decision of the group. In effect, he is responsible for discerning the discernment! This is an area that pastors tell me is often the most difficult for them to grasp. How can they balance the responsibility for the final outcome with the enabling and freeing they are to do? There are two approaches that I often find operating. Pastors express them this way:

1. I will listen carefully, respectfully, prayerfully to what my people say, that is, to the wisdom of the group, weigh it against my own wisdom and experience, and then do what I believe to be best for all concerned.

2. I will listen carefully, respectfully, prayerfully to what my people say, that is, to the wisdom of the group, and then do what they call me to even though it is quite different from what I would have decided if the choice were mine.

It is not, however, that simple. Neither of these approaches provides the total answer. A balance is called for that combines the wisdom of the group, pastoral responsibility and accountability, and the "let go" mentality to the degree that is appropriate. As spiritual leader the pastor too must grow in that holy virtue of disinterestedness. Futrell writes:

> Leaders who invite collegial participation in making decisions will recognize when their own feelings and desires must be let go for the good of the community. Such leaders will not be threatened by admitting their own limitations and calling on the strength and talents of others.
> . . . the leader who truly listens to community members will also be open to persuasion to change his or her mind. (5)

But it also works the other way around, as the author notes:

> One of the qualities to be desired in a leader is the ability to recognize the signs of the time—to be able to see new demands created by new situations and to lead sometimes reluctant community members in accepting needed adaptations and changes. (6)

Add to the reality of this dynamic the responsibility for orthodoxy and accountability to diocesan policy and the bishop. How can the pastor put it all together? He must learn to take the wisdom of the group and reflect on it in relationship to doctrine, policy, privileged information, and accountability to church authority. Then if the discerned decision is not contrary to any of the above, even if it is not to his liking, it may well be the call of the Spirit for him to surrender to the wisdom of the group.

Obviously, if there are serious reasons for not confirming the decision, his responsibility demands that he not confirm it. However, it seems appropriate that he share, as completely as possible, his reasons for this action. It might also be wise to invite the group to enter into a dialogue with him and so, in effect, to discern his discernment!

As a member of a council, board, or staff, the pastor wears two hats. He is the pastor, but he is also a member of the group. As a member, he has all the rights of membership. He needs to share his wisdom, be a part of the reflective dialogue that takes place, admit his fears, share his dreams. As pastor, he has an additional role: he is to discern the discernment! In legal church language, this is called the right of veto. The pastor has it. That is fact. But the way he uses this right, and the language he uses to define it, will go a long way either to encourage and nourish shared decision or to discourage it from the outset.

I personally do not like to use the term *veto.* I think it has a negative connotation that hints at authoritarian righteousness. To identify this right and responsibility as the pastor's "right of approval" seems to be more in tune with both the concept and the role of the spiritual director in the tradition. It is an affirming of the group's attentiveness to the Spirit. Or, when the approval is denied, it is a way of calling the discerners to greater awareness and honesty.

When I teach groups to make decisions within this model, I develop a step-by-step process that includes a time when the spiritual leader is asked to "put on your pastor's hat." Then as pastor, he is asked if he has any nonnegotiables. Let's say, for example, that a parish council is in the process of considering a proposal to identify additional staff. Two recommendations have been presented: one for a youth minister and the other for a liturgist/music minister. Adequate data has been presented, and prayerful reflection and shared wisdom have brought the group to a general agreement that it would not be possible to add both positions at this time. There also seems to be a leaning toward the liturgist/music minister.

Up to this point, the pastor has been very much a part of the group discussion, sharing his concerns, offering his insights and experiences like everyone else. Now, as the group gets closer to the final decision, he is asked to speak as pastor. He might say something like this:

> I realize that the cost of two staff positions could be a problem. I'm willing to go either way with that, although, obviously, I'd prefer that both be added. If we do come to see the importance of both at this time, I would certainly be willing to discuss possibilities

for cutting back in other areas so as not to increase the budget too much. The rest of the staff is also willing to make that effort.

I would also be comfortable with adding only one, provided that the one added is the youth minister. This is my nonnegotiable at this point in my thinking and praying about our vision for our parish and our needs as staff to bring about that vision.

The pastor would then explain his reasons. The explanation might deal with such things as clearly identified needs, the goals of the council itself, diocesan policy, and so on. The dialogue, prayerful reflection, and shared wisdom that would follow might persuade the pastor to change his position by opening up for him new and deeper insights. But if his position remains unaltered, it is to be respected and accepted by the council for what it is: the pastor's right and responsibility.

When that step is completed, the pastor can take off his pastor's hat and become a member again. (He never, of course, takes off his "spiritual leader" hat!) But the deliberations that follow will take into account what happened during the discussion of his nonnegotiables. This prevents the situation in which the pastor will be forced to use his veto power or refuse his approval.

The burden of good pastoring cannot simply be placed on the spiritual leader. There is a dynamic that must be alive and well if leadership is to be fruitful and successful. Among the most heartrending appeals spoken by Jesus were those in which He pleaded for understanding and presence:

> Have I been with you all this time . . . and you still do not know me?
> *John 14:9*

> Had you not the strength to keep awake one hour?
> *Mark 14:37*

All of us, pastors and people alike, long for acceptance. We long to be known and treasured; we need to be listened to and affirmed. All of us, pastors and people alike, look to one another for models of prayerfulness and holiness. We seek the Lord in each other's lives and attitudes, words and presence. To be a spiritual leader in a shared wisdom model of church is to enter into this dynamic and to call one's people to the dynamic.

So what does this model say to pastors? I think its message is clear: Be our leaders, our pastors. Shepherd us as you walk the journey with us. Model Gospel values in the midst of our shared struggle. Call us to a growing awareness of what it means to be Christian. Call us to prayer, to worship, to healing, to justice. Be our pastors, our *spiritual* leaders!

People today long for deeper intimacy with their God. The call of the Council that we be holy is being heard. The Spirit is placing in our hearts and our minds deep yearnings for new insights into Scripture, for more meaningful prayer. We are learning to talk to our God, to touch our God. And we are learning to listen to our God and respond to that tender yet persistent touch that is His way with us in all the areas of our lives.

I am convinced that the Spirit is preparing the church for a new recognition of the wider use of the gift of discernment. The holiness to which people feel called is leading them to discover in their own lives the movement and the call of the Spirit. As that continues to happen they will soon come to be at home with the God of the Gathering.

So, to pastors, to all of you who take up the challenge of spiritual leadership, I say: Leadership is critical. Pastoring is needed. Call us to that awareness of the Spirit within us. Be willing to share with us the God who touches you deeply and speaks to you and calls you. Let us know your struggles to respond, to hear, to understand. Be one with us in our efforts to be and to build church.

But even as you are one with us, call us when we forget what we are about. Bring us back to our commitment to share wisdom and to hear and respect wisdom. Don't, please, become part of the power struggle! Teach us to let go even as you struggle to learn the same lesson!

As we will fail at times, so will you. We understand that. Healing will always be a part of the journey. Allow us to heal you even as we turn so often to you in need of healing. Let us be and build church together.

We need you to care, to call, to challenge, to heal, to lead. We need you to love us!

Focus Questions for Chapter 6

1. Consider your lived experience of church leadership.

What ideas in this chapter reflect your experience of "pastor"?

_____

_____

_____

_____

_____

_____

What ideas in this chapter are new to you? Are confusing? Are questionable?

_____

_____

_____

_____

_____

_____

2. Reflect on and discuss the implications of the role of spiritual leader for your pastor and for your group.

_____

_____

_____

_____

_____

_____

N.B.: Honesty and sensitivity will be especially important to this discussion. It is necessary that we, priest and people together, grow in this model and support each other in that process.

Practical Implications

It seems obvious that in order to follow the concepts I have presented, there will have to be some organizational adjustments as well as the attitudinal ones I have already identified. Structures need to be evolved and developed that will support the efforts being made to receive the gift of the Spirit as the various decision-making groups seek to be and to build church.

I would like, therefore, to look at the structural and organizational implications of this shared wisdom model. To do this it seems appropriate to consider two broad categories of personnel:

1. The planners and policy developers: boards, councils, senates, and so on
2. The implementers: administrators, teams, faculties, and so on

THE PLANNERS

Let us start with the planners. These are groups that have typically been defined as policy makers and recognized as advisory to bishops and pastors. In the educational ministry, superintendents of schools, principals, and religious education vicars and coordinators have usually been defined as being accountable to such groups for the implementation of their decisions. These boards and councils have been largely lay in membership and have been viewed as somehow being representative of the parish, diocese, or parent community that typically elects them to the position. In some vague way, such boards and councils have usually seen themselves as being accountable to that constituency.

There are six major areas within the category of planners that I believe need to be considered for systems implications and adjustment. They are:

1. The purpose for which the group exists
2. The development of criteria for membership in the group
3. The responsibilities of the group
4. The relationship that this group has to those not a part of its membership
5. Formation and in-service
6. Meeting procedures and skills

Purpose

During the years since Vatican II much has been said about having the laity involved in church. We have recognized the value and the importance of their talents and their experience, especially in the areas of business procedures, development, and public relations. We have also come to recognize that church belongs to all of us and we all need to share the responsibility for it. Boards and councils seemed a way to do this. So we asked people to share their talents, to gift the church with their time, to bring to church decision making their experience of "worldly wisdom" in terms of organizational skills. We have called upon them to accept serious responsibilities for parishes and for the dioceses through these various decision-making structures.

All of that has been good so far as it has gone. Or at least a great deal of it has been good. One thing that such efforts have accomplished is the identification of countless numbers of people who are willing and able and even anxious to be involved in church. As I have said elsewhere, however, some people who have been brought to these roles are not equipped, trained, or even suited for such ministry commitments. It is my strong conviction that we must begin to clearly state the purpose of boards and councils but not in vague terms of service to the church and acceptance of the call of the Council to be involved, and certainly not in terms of "keeping the church honest" or in any sense of "getting" someone or something. I believe that we must state the primary purpose of decision-making groups in church as:

to build, strengthen, and nourish church.

Criteria for Membership

Given this statement of purpose, it becomes clear that a call to serve on a board or council or senate is, in fact, a call to ministry, to the being and the building of church. From this clarity it is possible to develop criteria in the areas of—

- spiritual growth,
- motivation,
- commitment,
- skills and talents.

I have defined "building church" as involvement in ministry and have maintained, therefore, that one cannot be thus involved without "being church," that is, giving oneself to the spiritual journey. This, then, becomes the first criterion for membership. Any recruitment efforts will need to begin with this call to holiness. No, we are not looking for perfect people, but we are looking for those who are willing to make a commitment to their personal spirituality. It is this willingness to grow in the Lord, to commit oneself to the journey toward wholeness and holiness, that needs to be stressed. Admittedly, this approach could scare a lot of folks away! There must be the assurance that (1) spiritual growth is a journey (not a completed state of perfection!) and (2) all members will share the struggle and help one another on the journey.

Motivation also needs to be considered. A person should not think of this ministry chiefly as a means of growing in holiness. It may well happen, and I believe should happen, that board and council members find themselves growing in holiness. However, the primary motivation must be the ministry of decision making in a church model. The potential candidates must recognize that a response to this call will place them in a dynamic that will involve personal growth, deeper insights into church, greater involvement in human problems, new understandings of the gift of the Spirit to the church, and the inevitable struggles, both their own and those of all the others called to be and to build church! There may well be secondary motivations, for example, the expertise of a professional person such as a lawyer or CPA, but the primacy of ministry is critical and, I believe, nonnegotiable. Obviously, "political" power is an inappropriate motivation.

Then there is the matter of commitment. More than anything this needs to be realistically stated. In all too many parishes the few are so overcommitted that time and energy simply give out and things do not get done, or get done poorly, or, saddest of all, get done with a spirit of martyrdom or in great anger. Often, I fear, such overcommitment has tragic effects on family life and commitments as well. One of the greatest pastoral challenges that I see in the renewing church is that of disallowing overcommitment on the part of generous, well-meaning people. Even in small parishes, I do not believe that any one person should be allowed to make multiple ministry commitments. I recognize the problems of limited resources and the apathy on the part of so many who simply do not come forward, thus leaving so much to the few. But I also wonder if we do not affirm that apathy by allowing the many to be served by the few. Perhaps if some things just did not happen for a while, the point could be made that other folks were needed to make them happen! And even if that was not the result, it is far better, I believe, to have less going on than to cause people to suffer ministry burnout or to be responsible for inordinately absent spouses and parents, thus keeping them from their primary vocation, the nurturing of their own families. So, in calling people to this ministry, it is only fair to provide a clear indication of the kind of time and psychic commitment that will be expected.

Spiritual growth, exemplary motivation, and informed commitment, however, do not lessen the need for skills and talent. Again, recruitment procedures must give people a realistic way of judging their competence for this ministry. If a person is terrified of speaking in a group or even fairly uncomfortable in such a setting, that is most likely an indicator that such ministry will not be appropriate. The model demands a process that will enable people to test their skills, talents, and aptitudes before even considering a nomination. Nor are we simply talking about group skills. Depending on the kind of group (is it a school board? a diocesan senate? a parish council?), other talents and experiences will be needed. These must be identified and then a process provided so that potential nominees will be empowered to match their own gifts with the needs of the parish or diocese.

Responsibilities of the Group

I am more and more convinced that we have caused much of the confusion about the distinctions between the role of the board or council and that of the administrators by the responsibilities we have built into the structures. It is both my experience and my intuitive conviction that we could clear up a great deal of the confusion if we would define the board or council responsibilities as—

- policy development and recommended adoption,
- planning and goal setting,
- development and stewardship.

All other responsibilities and procedures would flow from these three major areas. Such a distinction, I believe, would keep the boards and councils doing what they should be doing while also keeping them clearly out of the administration of the parish, school, or diocese.

Relationships

Key to the implementation of a model of shared wisdom is a mutual trust at all levels: board/council to pastor/administrators/staff, pastor/administrators/ staff to board/council, board/council to constituencies, constituencies to board/council. Trust is not just something that happens or that can simply be willed. It must be seen as desirable, worked at, handled with care, and nourished consistently. Trust recognizes and accepts the roles, the talents, the experiences, the responsibilities, and the needs of all those involved. It also recognizes and accepts the human limitations, the past histories, and the newness of the challenges. Trust frees and empowers. It allows those involved to live and minister and fail and succeed in the real world where great things will happen. But dumb mistakes will be made, mediocrity will get in the way, misunderstandings and unclear expectations will cause difficulties, and judgments will not always be accurate. Trust allows us to accept the realities of the human condition.

Administrators and staff members need to see themselves as the professionals they are. It is their responsibility to bring to the board or council the data, the insights, the lived experience of ministry, the knowledge that flows from their roles, and the wisdom that is theirs. Then they must translate all of the above into policy recommendations, program implementation, organizational structures, and proposed directions for the future. It is equally their responsibility to respect the discerned decisions and directions of the board or council, to implement policies, to develop the agreed-upon goals, and to be accountable to the board or council for such implementation and program development.

On the other hand, the board or council must be willing to accept and respect the professional wisdom, insights, and expertise of the administrators and the staff. It needs to turn to them for the data and ministerial experience that will enable the decisions arrived at by the discerning group to reflect not only the group's needs and concerns but also the needs of the administrators who will implement the decisions.

Then there are relationships that need to be fostered between the board or council and the parish or the parent community that typically selects the decision-making groups in the parish. Members of the larger community must respect the process of decision making and allow the board or council to accomplish its goals. They must also accept their responsibility to respond when the board or council seeks their wisdom.

At the same time, the decision makers must not lose sight of the very real fact that they are called to gather the wisdom from the larger community from time to time. They must also feel themselves in some way accountable to that parish or parent community and develop procedures for accountability.

Committees, commissions, and task forces, whether connected to the board or council or to the administrators or staff, need to see themselves functioning within a defined area and responsible for specific tasks. Without this awareness it is easy to develop an approach that resembles the tail wagging the dog! These groups must be willing to take direction and to work within the parameters of that direction. Leaders of such groups, however, must be able to give them sufficient latitude so that creativity will not be stifled.

Genuine leadership, whether at the level of the board or council or the administrators and staff, is leadership that directs, frees, enables, affirms, challenges, calls, and sometimes redirects. But it also has the grace and the good sense to leave individuals free to develop their own methods and approaches. This, too, flows from that attitude of trust. The gifted leader can trust what a group or an individual does even if the approach is not the one the leader would have chosen.

Nor is this an irresponsible approach. Evaluation is a critically important component of this model. Trust does not preclude professional evaluation. This is especially significant when we come to understand evaluation as a process committed to the growth of those people being evaluated and the improvement of programs, goals, and procedures. Accountability and evaluation must be built into the model. It is not, of course, that we attempt to evaluate the workings of the Spirit in the situation but rather that we seek to evaluate the individual's or the group's sensitivity to the Spirit and then the adequacy of tasks accomplished and decisions made. Failures as well as inadequacy of response call not for reproof or retaliation, but rather for challenge, support, assistance, and direction in this ongoing process of being and building church.

Formation and In-service

A shared wisdom model of church will not happen automatically or without intent, training, prayer, and practice. Formation and in-service are essential to the model. Programs and procedures need to be developed that will reach people both before they accept a nomination and after they are elected. As ongoing formation and in-service are expected of the professional minister, so it will be expected of those called to the ministry of decision making.

The first thing that is necessary in the prenomination process is a way to make people aware of this ministry. At both the diocesan and the parish levels adequate information needs to be made available about the model, the spirituality involved, and the theology and ecclesi-ology that are operative in the model. What is critical here is that the call is clearly one that is more than political, practical, prestigious, or even just vaguely religious or generous. It is a call to minister to the people of God, to create and to nourish church—a call that is possible only within the personal call to holiness.

The prenomination process also needs to allow people to get in touch with their own giftedness and the needs of the parish or the diocese. This enables them to match their gifts with the needs of the church.

A third consideration before nominations are accepted is a pro-gram that will clarify roles, relationships, and responsibilities as well as expectations. Once on a board or council a person should encounter very few surprises. Realism is critical to commitment. The wide-eyed romantic seldom has the tested endurance called for in this experience we call shared decision making in church! Of course, there will be unknowns. Some of them will be delightful and rewarding. Some will hinge on devastation. But at least the crippling effects of disillusion-ment can be offset by honest explanations and the sharing of lived experiences with those who are already involved and committed.

Once elected, a person is expected to take part in various in-service programs and procedures. These include experiences that will help develop the following:
- An understanding of the mission and philosophy of the church
- A way to internalize that mission and philosophy
- Good meeting procedures and skills
- Techniques for forums and consultations
- Conflict management skills
- Evaluation skills
- Public relation techniques

Much of this will just be a matter of reminding people about skills they are already familiar with and allowing them to practice these skills. But such skill formation should never be taken for granted or ignored as not needed.

The same is true for the formation process. It must be a continual program and process that will include prayer experiences, sharing of faith stories, Eucharistic celebrations, periodic days or hours of reflec-tion to support the prayerful atmosphere of the meetings, and social gatherings that will help build the faith community.

Meeting Procedures and Skills

A shared decision model will evolve a distinct methodology in relation to the preparation for and the implementation of its meetings.

Always the consideration that will be first in the minds and planning of the organizers will be the presence of the Spirit and how to assure that this presence is respected, treasured, and freed to operate in the hearts and minds of all the members.

Lead time is an important consideration. Annual planning for decisions to be made and actions to be taken allows the group to so plan agendas that there will seldom be the kind of bind that forces the group to hurry any decision through. There will always be exceptions. But that is exactly what they should be: exceptions! Emergencies will arise, as I have noted elsewhere, and these will force the group to come to an immediate decision. It is usually best to avoid a discerned decision in such situations and to be satisfied, at least for the present, to move with a simple majority vote. Let me repeat: Such emergencies are exceptions and therefore are unusual rather than usual.

Part of the secret to success in all meetings is the preparation of the agenda not only in terms of clarity but also in terms of back-up materials and time of distribution. Sufficient time for study and reflection must be provided. It goes without saying that as the organizers of a meeting are responsible for developing a meaningful agenda, providing adequate data, and getting it to the members in advance, the members of the group are equally responsible for spending the necessary time studying and reflecting prayerfully on the agenda and the materials provided. They have been given all of this material so that each person may arrive at the meeting with his or her piece of the wisdom—a wisdom that has been prayed through, thought out, and is now ready to be shared with the others.

Two things unique to this model must be considered in structuring a meeting:

1. The use of a procedure that allows time for reflection and prayer before sharing wisdom

2. The inclusion of times of reflective prayer after the wisdom has been shared

There are other common-sense considerations that need to be thought through and planned for, not least among them the environmental aspects of where a meeting takes place and how the room is set up and the atmosphere established.

Skills for sharing wisdom are not that difficult to learn. However, for most of us, it is not just a matter of learning skills, although we may need to do that. It is more importantly an ongoing task of practicing what we have learned and committed ourselves to. Because all of us require reminders, assistance, and support if we are to consistently be functional in meeting situations, we need good leadership and we also need to help each other so that we will be called to the kind of behavior that we desire.

One of the skills necessary in this model is the skill of consensus decision making, previously discussed on pages 51-53. It is critical that the group recognize that a consensus decision will not always be possible. Before the process is even begun, the group must agree to accept a majority decision if necessary, and to accept it as the will of the Spirit! This is not the same as agreeing to go with the majority and to support the decision. The shared wisdom model asks group members, in advance of the decision, to agree to see and to embrace the decision of the majority as the discerned decision, the will of the Spirit, the voice of the Lord being heard by this group at this time over this issue. Only this position will bring the peace and contentment that is the indicator of the gift of the Spirit.

Richard P. McBrien in *Catholicism* provides criteria for recognizing the presence of a discerned decision. For some reason, he chooses to state them negatively, but what he says deserves our consideration.

> Although we can never be absolutely certain that we are indeed responding to the Spirit, there are certain *negative criteria* by which obviously false responses can be exposed: (1) If the discernment process does not issue forth in the classic "fruits" of the Spirit—love, joy, peace, patient endurance, kindness, generosity, faith, mildness, and chastity (Gal. 5:22-23)—it is not "of the Spirit." (2) If the discernment process leads to doctrinal or moral positions which are clearly inconsistent with the doctrinal positions of the church and/or with recognized norms of biblical and theological scholarship, it is not "of the Spirit." (3) If the discernment process intensifies the isolation and even spiritual eccentricities of those involved in it rather than enhancing the life of the whole Body of Christ (Eph. 4:15-16), it is not "of the Spirit." (4) If the discernment process ignores pertinent information, rejects the counsel of others who have knowledge and experience in the matter at hand, and formulates its judgments by imposition rather than by corporate reflection, it is not "of the Spirit." (1)

THE IMPLEMENTERS

The systems implications identified in this section include efforts to create a climate or a structure, as well as skills and a support system, that will make possible a discerned decision. Such a decision is one in which the fruits of the Spirit will be experienced, respect for church doctrine and norms will be evident, and the community—the Body of Christ—will be nourished. Corporate reflection during this process will include shared wisdom as well as the counsel of others who are knowledgeable.

People in leadership and professional roles must be as aware of purpose, as clear about criteria for hiring staff and faculty, as alert to responsibilities and relationships, as definite about formation and in-service, and as skilled in meeting procedures as any member of the board or council. In fact, my experience indicates that it is the professional staff that sets the tone for the others involved in the school or parish. The responsibility to model behavior is a grave one.

For many years now we have had this understanding of modeling behavior in our philosophy of Catholic schools. In the early seventies the concept of a Catholic school as a Christian educational community resulted in many of the things I'm calling for in these systems implications. Teachers were called to model a behavior that matched what they were teaching in religion classes. This approach called for the development of criteria for hiring faculty members and selecting administrators so that such a goal could be accomplished. Motivation was related to the development of the faith community in the school, and commitment was broader than the teaching of a subject or a grade. Skills were developed and nourished, especially the group skills that would nourish the growth of the community. Relationships were stressed—relationships to children, to each other, and to the parent community. We came to recognize that teaching, as a ministry, was a call to holiness—a call to build church, to nourish church, and to strengthen church while being professionally competent.

These same kinds of considerations need to be evident in the choices that are made about hiring staff at any level of parish or diocesan life. And those people who seek employment in church need to realize that such employment is, in fact, more than employment; it is commitment to ministry, commitment to church. (This is *not* to say they should be less professionally competent or less justly reimbursed!) Those who are in positions of authority and are making decisions about personnel need to remind themselves that ministry is the primary criterion. The first question must be: Is this person (teacher, pastoral assistant, coach, catechist, music minister) in touch with this role as a call to ministry, a call that demands spiritual formation and a commitment to be and to build church? It is easy to lose sight of this dimension when the search is for a sharp upper-grade science and math teacher, a professional musician, or whatever!

Obviously, while inclusion in and commitment to ministry is primary, it is not enough. Staff positions do need to be filled by skilled people who are trained in the field in which they will function. This is where job descriptions are so important. So are clearly defined and discussed job expectations which flow from the job descriptions. Among those expectations will be that of working with other members of the staff, the faculty, the council, and the board to build church in the parish and to strengthen faith community in the school and religious education programs.

And, as with board and council members, staff members require in-service, formation programs, and spiritual development experiences. Participation in times of reflection, in the Eucharist and other prayer experiences, as well as in social gatherings, needs to be a clearly stated expectation for all members of the staff.

Why the social gatherings? I believe that community—be that faith, parish, school, diocese, or family community—simply will not happen if celebration is not a part of the effort. For some reason the renewing church has become incredibly grim. I suspect that it may be because we have taken on so much of the character of the corporation that must be efficient, time and cost effective, and always professional in conduct.

Church is a call to the kingdom. Granted, the fullness of that kingdom is not to be found here and now, but the preview is often so uninviting! Jesus modeled a spirit of celebration that we easily overlook. He was big into parties! Consider, if you will, His presence at the wedding feast, the picnics, and His dinner party, and His willingness to stop for supper at the local restaurant.

To everyone involved in church ministry it seems appropriate to say: If you are really into following the Lord, to making His presence known, to building His church, inform your calendar! Plan some fun times, some time to celebrate that reality. The ability of the members of a board or council or staff to celebrate who they are and what they are about is a necessity for the health of the community. This ability reflects their understanding of the Good News and is a sign of the joy with which they are committed to being and building church!

Focus Questions for Chapter 7

1. Consider the statement: "The primary purpose of decision-making groups in church is to build, strengthen, and nourish church."

How does this statement match your experience of your council, board, or staff?

_____

_____

How does the statement fit your understanding of decision-making groups in church?

_____

_____

2. Reflect on how people become members of your council, board, or staff.

What are the criteria for membership? _____

_____

_____

In what ways are your criteria adequate?_____

_____

_____

In what ways are they inadequate?_____

_____

_____

3. Reflect on the relationships among the total parish and the staff, council, or board.

In what ways are these relationships healthy and productive?

_____

_____

_____

In what ways are they inadequate or destructive?

_____

_____

_____

4. Recall your first year as a member of your council, board, or staff.

What was your orientation to the role and the task? _____

_____

_____

What was missing in your orientation? _____

_____

_____

Have ongoing formation and in-service been a part of your experience? What form have they taken?

_____

_____

5. Spend some time thinking about your meetings.

What works? _____

_____

_____

What doesn't work?_____

_____

_____

Why do you think some procedures or strategies don't work?

_____

_____

6. Reflect on the role of the leader(s) in your group.

What promotes effective leadership? _____

_____

_____

What hinders or limits effective leadership? _____

_____

_____

What could make a difference in how effective a leader is?

_____

_____

_____

Procedures

The areas that remain to be dealt with are structural and are related to the design of support systems for the model. They are:

1. Identification of nominees
2. Initial formation and in-service
3. Ongoing formation and in-service
4. Group leadership
5. Agenda planning
6. Meeting skills
7. Long-range planning and goal setting
8. Hearing from the publics
9. Evaluation

IDENTIFICATION OF NOMINEES

As I have described the model it should be evident that some special attention needs to be given to how people become members of boards or councils. I am increasingly convinced that the best route is one of self-nomination that is confirmed through a process that allows people to make choices for the kingdom. In Chapter 4 I discussed what I consider to be unfortunate ways of identifying nominees. Let me now offer a possible approach that would seem more in tune with the call of the Spirit to be and to build church.

Like everything else about this model, the process of identifying nominees is not a simple one that can be done without much thought or planning or commitment of time and effort. It involves a number of steps. They are:

1. Providing the people of the parish or diocese with adequate information about a shared wisdom model of church and the concept of involvement in it as a call to holiness and to ministry

2. Planning a process whereby interested people can examine their own gifts and talents and be helped to match them with the needs of the parish or diocese

3. Providing a discerning experience for those who feel themselves called—an experience that will include a consultation with some member of the staff whose task it will be to confirm the decision or redirect the possible nominee to other forms of ministry

4. Initiating the actual self-nomination procedure

The first step, providing adequate information, will take whatever form is tried and true within the parish or diocese. A diocese may choose to use its diocesan paper, a special pamphlet prepared for this purpose and distributed to all the parishes, a radio or television spot, or a letter from the local ordinary. A parish might devote homilies to this topic, feature it in the parish bulletin, send a letter or pamphlet to every family in the parish, or do a presentation for all those who might be interested. How it is done is not important as long as the message reaches as many people as possible and invites them to at least consider the possibility of such a call.

Once people have some understanding of what the model is about, the next step is to gather those who think they might be interested. This can be done in one night or spread out over a series of evenings. One parish I worked with scheduled this part of the process for the Wednesday evenings in Lent, for example. The purpose of this step is to provide a way in which people can look at their own gifts and talents, those things that they do well and enjoy doing, and then see if their gifts match the challenge of the shared wisdom model. One obvious area of concern would be the potential nominees' interest in personal spiritual growth. Another would be the degree of ease with which they participate in group process. Another would be their motivation for being interested. The sessions would need to be designed around these areas. The final session, or the end of the evening if there is just one session, would be a prayerful and personal guided discernment in which each person would be enabled to make a tentative decision about a possible call to ministry in the parish or diocese. Materials for doing this discernment are found in Appendix I, pages 140–43.

Why do I say tentative? Because a discerned decision always needs to be confirmed or challenged. This was the role of the spiritual director in the tradition. It extends now to the spiritual leader or some member of the staff who will meet with each person who has discerned a call. The meeting will be in the context of prayerful reflection and will either affirm the discernment or call the person to continued reflection.

If the decision is confirmed, the parishioner will be encouraged to submit a self-nomination form. Such a form will be designed to provide information for the people who will be doing the voting. It would probably look something like this:

I nominate myself for _____ because

_____. I feel that I would bring

_____ to this ministry.

Name _____

Other information that seems pertinent could also be requested, but the above is the most important.

Once the nominees are discerned, the process of final selection can vary according to the experience and expectations of the parish or diocese: election, appointment, or a combination of the two.

INITIAL FORMATION AND IN-SERVICE

Before becoming a working part of the group, the newly elected members will be expected to involve themselves in some initial formation and in-service. I see four things as critical to the newcomers' training. The first of these is an understanding of the importance not only of processing life but of learning the simple skills involved in doing so. And the best people to serve as the "teachers" of the experience will be members of the board or council who have learned this valuable spiritual art and are willing to share their own struggles with it, the growth they have experienced, and their insights and hopes.

Second, the newly elected members need to become familiar with the philosophy, mission, or charism of the group they are representing. Depending on the group, this may be a mission statement for the diocese or parish, the philosophy of the school, or the charism of the council or board itself. It is important that new members learn something of how the statement was developed and what its implications are for the operational values of the board or council. Then they need an opportunity to internalize the statement and claim it as their own.

Procedures and expectations are third on my list. Take nothing for granted. Clarify all procedures followed by the board or council and identify those expectations that apply to all members of the group. Part of this can be accomplished by a reflective study of the group's bylaws. Use of pages 120-24 of Appendix I is helpful for clarifying expectations.

Finally, an overview of meeting skills should be provided. This is especially necessary in this model since so many people coming on a board or council will be familiar with parliamentary procedures but will not be all that clear on how to function in a group that does not follow Robert's Rules. Materials are given on pages 125-28 of Appendix I to assist the group in skill development.

ONGOING FORMATION AND IN-SERVICE

Formation and in-service are necessary for all members of the board or council. There are many approaches to meeting this need. Some groups will devote fifteen to twenty minutes of every meeting to various activities of this kind. Others plan special meetings or even annual days or weekends for these experiences. Whatever the design, there are some things that always need to be included. In the formation area, periodic prayer experiences that are more than just an opening or closing prayer should be planned, as should an annual afternoon or day of reflection. It is usually best, by the way, to hold such a retreat away from the parish or the usual place of meeting. Although it can be difficult to get everyone, including the pastor, to be present for the entire day, that should be one of the expectations. There is a dynamic involved in such a day of prayer, a bonding that takes place. To have some members miss the experience is to lessen the long-range value for the entire group.

Planning for times of special reflection might be done by a resource person brought in for this purpose, but most groups have within their membership the people who can provide such services. Some samples of prayer experiences are offered in Appendix I (pages 108-10) to indicate the types of reflection that might be helpful. Obviously, most important to the success of such reflections will be how deeply they touch the people involved and how significantly they speak to where the group is in its own spiritual growth.

Critical to the shared wisdom model are two methods of getting in touch with both the God of individual lived experience and the God of the Gathering. They are faith sharing and theological reflection, terms that often frighten people. These experiences are not at all frightening; rather, they are very beautiful and grace-filled opportunities.

Faith sharing is exactly what it is called: a sharing of faith. It is taking any personal or group experience and, in the light of faith, seeking to connect that experience with the action of God in one's life. Then, out of that reflection, an individual shares his or her insights with the other members of the group. The reading and the reflection on pages 114-15 are provided for this purpose. Faith sharing can also be done with a scriptural passage as a starting point, relating that passage to personal and group experiences and sharing the insights. This is usually an extremely enriching experience for all involved because (1) it provides the opportunity for each person to do some prayerful reflection and thus get in touch with new insights and understandings of the action of the Lord in life situations and (2) it offers the richness and variety of the wisdom of other people.

Theological reflection is really not that different from faith sharing except that it will often start with some theological concept. Reflections for this purpose are found on pages 116-19 of Appendix I. These are based on:

- The God of the Gathering
- Ministry
- The gift of the Spirit
- The renewing church

These theological concepts are then reflected on in the light of an individual's lived experience. For example, while reflecting on the God of the Gathering, you would want to consider the presence of God in your family, in your parish, and in the world. Having established where He is to be experienced, you would then reflect on what the experience might be. In this case it would be your experience of God (1) in the gathering, (2) in bondedness, (3) in fragmentation, and (4) in healing. (Please keep in mind that the reflection pages in Appendix I are only samples and should be used only if they match your needs and the needs of your group.)

People need time and space to reflect prayerfully if they are to gain from such experiences. Given a day for such spiritual development this is not a problem. However, if such experiences are planned as part of a meeting, it would be necessary to distribute the reflection activities in advance of the meeting.

The dialogue that takes place after the personal reflection that prepares for faith sharing or theological reflection is always a sacred time and should be respected and treasured as such. It is not a time for debate but rather a time for listening with the ear of the heart. Obviously if some insight seems to be leading to untruth, the spiritual leader will want to provide some direction. But even in these cases, the confrontation must be extremely gentle and never dogmatic or demanding. Often just by questioning a person respectfully the leader can bring the person beyond the point of difficulty to the truth. Extreme care should be taken that a new idea is not automatically branded as untrue!

Allow me to offer some rules of thumb that apply to all those situations in which people are asked to move from personal reflection to group sharing. They are:

1. The leader should *always* tell members of the group that they will be asked to share their reflections, and should tell them *before* they do the reflecting.

2. Since many people find it difficult to share such personal information in a large group, the leader should begin the first round of sharing by suggesting that each person find one other person in the group to share with. Only after five or ten minutes of one-on-one sharing should the leader invite the large group dialogue.

3. The leader should remind the group that each person is to share only that part of his or her personal reflection that he or she feels comfortable sharing. No pressure should ever be placed on a person to reveal more than he or she wants to share.

4. The leader should model the behavior asked of the group by using his or her own personal reflections on the concept or issue as examples of what is to be done.

These are general guidelines for group reflection and sharing that work well for me in any group I'm directing. As a spiritual leader or facilitator works with a specific group, other guidelines may develop.

Central to our Catholic tradition is the celebration of Eucharist. It is in the breaking and sharing of the bread and cup that we are united with the Lord and with one another in sign and sacrament. It is hard to imagine a group of people who have committed themselves to the being and the building of church who would not recognize the significance of celebrating Eucharist together. Most often, of course, the celebration takes place within the context of the larger parish community, but there also needs to be special celebrations built around themes that relate to the purpose and the issues that unite the group, or perhaps even to the problems! Years ago, in the beginning of the Vatican II renewal, the Sisters of the Blessed Virgin Mary had a renewal chapter that they wisely called "Problems That Unite Us." That would make a great theme for a Eucharistic celebration in some parishes, dioceses, and religious communities! At least you wouldn't run out of ideas!

Often, and wisely, Eucharistic celebrations are combined with social celebrations: a meal, a picnic, or just an evening of being together for relaxation. This is an excellent time to include spouses in the celebration or, in the case of boards of education or school boards, to invite the faculty and the catechists. Community building is the process of binding people together in the real world in which they live. No group ever became a faith community by simply working together. Community development and bondedness flow from the combination of working, praying, and celebrating together.

One of my most significant experiences of community bondedness happened during the ten years I was on the staff of the Catholic School Office in Chicago. We were a large group, numbering well over fifty persons, but we were a faith community. Why? Because when we worked, we worked as if there was no tomorrow; when we prayed, we prayed like contemplatives; and when we celebrated, we had terrific parties!

There is also the whole area of professional in-service that must be provided for the council or board. Many dioceses provide all manner of in-service opportunities, and there are materials available through national offices and organizations. As with formation, in-service can be scheduled monthly as a part of the regular meeting, or special sessions can be scheduled for this purpose. The decision about what should be provided for the group will flow from the needs of the group and the types of tasks and issues they are involved with in any given year of operation. Some general areas that need to be covered, perhaps in a three- or four-year cycle, are:

- Policy development
- Goal setting
- Long-range planning
- Development, public relations, and stewardship
- Evaluation
- Consultations
- Open forums
- Public relations

Related to in-service is the area of group behaviors, meeting skills, and the general dynamics that evolve as the group works together. No amount of goodwill, clarity of expectations, commitment to the group, or even prayer will guarantee the absence of periodic malfunctions. People are people, and church groups are made up of people. It is not a sign of failure or a lack of commitment when a group realizes that things are not going as smoothly as desired. The failure comes in the unwillingness to admit difficulties or to deal with them in a productive way. Two things need to be evaluated from time to time: group behaviors and the operational level of the philosophy of shared wisdom. Possible ways of doing this are provided in Appendix I, pages 130–31 and 145. The annual retreat day may well be a good time to schedule such experiences. However, if problems arise anytime during the year, they should be dealt with as soon as possible so a group will not be crippled by dysfunctional behavior or negative attitudes.

GROUP LEADERSHIP

In a parliamentary model the chairperson is, in the very best sense of the word, a controlling person. This is not true in the shared wisdom model. Here the leader needs to be one who can empower people, enable process, and confront dysfunctional behavior—no small role description, but not an impossible one to meet.

To empower people is to free them to be true to their own thoughts and feelings, to give them the opportunity to think these through, and to help them feel valued within the group. It is to allow every member of the group equal or at least adequate time to share wisdom with the rest of the group. A shared wisdom model leader will understand the importance of encouraging participation. Often the most important skill the leader needs is that of gently but firmly preventing the talkers in the group from dominating the conversation. Such a leader will seek the information and wisdom of those who are hesitant to volunteer their insights and feelings. It is the responsibility of the leader to track not only the agenda but also the ideas that are expressed. For some reason, some people's wisdom tends to fall to the floor! They say something and it's as though they never said it. The discussion goes on without any reference to what has been shared. We say that these people "plop." It is a devastating experience for the one who "plops," and that is reason enough to do something about the situation. But in addition, the group loses a piece of wisdom. The leader, then, has the double responsibility of getting this person back into the group and retrieving the wisdom that has been lost. Usually a simple "I think we just missed something that Chuck said. Chuck, please run that by us again" will accomplish the dual purpose of making Chuck feel valued and present to the group while bringing his wisdom to the group's attention.

Groups often become tense or weary for reasons that they do not completely understand. Or a member of the group will be having these negative feelings and not realize that others share the same concerns or uneasiness. The leader needs to be attentive to group and individual feelings. The purpose of such attentiveness is lost, however, unless the feelings are expressed. The leader will find many ways to express group feelings. Sometimes it will be best to appropriate these feelings to oneself and test them out to see if others are sharing them. Other times it will be best to simply ask persons what they are feeling, or if they can get in touch with why they are angry or hurt or unwilling to participate. Time spent getting in touch with feelings is far from wasted. Feelings can hinder a group from doing much of anything if they are left unattended.

The shared wisdom model leader is also called upon to be an enabler of process. Although the rules of parliamentary procedure will not be used except perhaps for the most routine issues on the agenda, this does not imply any lack of order or discipline in the meeting procedure. While all members of the group need to become familiar with process skills, it is the leader who needs to be the most skilled. He or she will lead the group to initiate new topics and ideas, will model both seeking and giving information, will call for clarification at the least hint of confusion in the discussion, and will consistently track those who stray from the topic. The ability to summarize and synthesize are crucial. Among the most often used skills is that of consensus testing to give the group a sense of where it is in the process. Another skill that the leader will need to develop is helping the group achieve a sense of closure on issues. Closely related to this skill is the understanding of the many ways in which a group makes decisions. It is not merely by vote! Groups often decide not to decide by ignoring an issue. Or they allow one or two of their members to make the decision by not confronting the kind of behavior that causes this to happen or by just not participating in the decision. The leader needs to recognize these situations and in each case call the members of the group to honesty and behavior modification.

This responsibility relates to the final skill that I believe is necessary for the leader of a shared wisdom model: confronting dysfunctional behavior kindly, clearly, and consistently. My position on such behavior is a strong one. Given what the model seeks to do, that is, allow the wisdom of the Spirit of God to be available to the group, it is my conviction that any dysfunctional behavior that prevents the members of the group from sharing their own wisdom or hearing the wisdom of one another is, by definition, a sin against the Spirit. As such, it must be confronted. I also believe that any person who malfunctions must be confronted, whether that person is the oldest, most respected member of the group, the pastor, or whoever. Obviously, such confrontation will initially be done in private. It is my almost universal experience that people who malfunction in groups have very little if any idea of the devastating effect that their behavioral patterns have on the group. So they need to be told—not scolded or threatened or belittled, but just informed, kindly and clearly, with some examples of the dysfunctional behavior given. Then there would follow a discussion of why this kind of behavior is a problem in the group and how the person might be helped to change.

How does a group "find" such a leader? I strongly recommend the use of discernment for the selection of leadership. It must be understood that the "perfect leader" may not be found, but the discernment process allows for the identification of that person in the group who seems to have the greatest number of skills needed and the greatest potential and willingness to develop these skills.

AGENDA PLANNING

It is my experience that one of the most important tools available to the meeting process is the agenda. Of course, the agenda must be well developed if it is to be significant. The purpose of an agenda is two-fold: to allow the members to reflect in advance so that they will have their wisdom ready to share when they come to the meeting, and to provide an organized way to move through the meeting.

If the agenda is to allow people to reflect, it must be complete enough to guide them through their reflection. Agendas written as one-word items are seldom useful. Sentence agendas or even paragraph agendas are much better. My own preference is a topical agenda with questions for consideration and reflection given under each topic. However the agenda is organized, it is often helpful to include in the agenda packet additional information that will help people in the necessary reflecting. It is also critical that the agenda packets be distributed well in advance of the meeting, certainly no less than three or four days before the scheduled meeting date.

Any issue on the agenda that needs to be discerned will have to be scheduled with sufficient flexibility to allow time for reflection during the meeting. Great amounts of time can be saved at meetings if reports are submitted in writing and sent out in advance with the agenda so that everyone comes prepared to move right into the discussion of the reports. This is also a good approach to the minutes of the previous meeting, the year-to-date financial report, and even some parts of the administrators' reports.

I am often asked if everything a board or council deals with must be discerned in the shared wisdom model. Obviously there are routine matters that can be—and should be—handled very efficiently with a simple voting procedure. Only major decisions such as policy, goals, approval of budget, selection of administrators and group leaders, and significant changes in program or procedures lend themselves to the discernment process. An interesting phenomenon begins to happen, however, as a group experiences the grace of discerned decisions. While not all the steps will be taken in less important areas, much of the attitudinal qualities of the shared wisdom philosophy will gradually be felt in all areas of the group's experience. There will be less competitiveness, less controlling behavior, a more reflective and prayerful approach to even the smallest details, and an increasing awareness of and respect for the God of the Gathering and the wisdom that comes from each member of the group. It is as this begins to happen that a real sense of church emerges in the group. At the same time, ministry becomes more than a term; it becomes the lived experience of the members of the group.

One thing that those who plan agendas must keep in mind is the differing needs of introverts and extroverts. Introverts think while they think, so they always need time and space and *quiet* in which to do their thinking. Extroverts think when they talk, so they always need time and space and *people* with whom to do their thinking. This has a great deal to do with how a meeting is planned. All of us who chair and facilitate meetings know the scenario only too well. You give the group members a new topic to consider and then ask that they take five or ten minutes to reflect prayerfully on the topic. The introverts are delighted. The extroverts cheat! They find someone to talk to! The secret to success is to give the extroverts some way to "talk" without disturbing the introverts. This is why I make such wide use of reflection sheets. I hand out simple ones with just one or two questions for reflection. The introverts hardly look at them but the extroverts write their thoughts, another way for them to "talk." There is, however, another step in the process. Although writing is helpful for the extroverts, it is really not enough. So, after the five or ten minutes of silent reflection, I ask the group to split into groups of two and allow the pairs to talk through their reflections for another five or ten minutes. Such a simple and painless procedure allows everyone "think" time and enhances the quality of the discussion that follows.

MEETING SKILLS

There are so many! Probably the most critical skills for the shared wisdom model are those that foster attentive listening and respect for one another's wisdom. Developing these skills takes a lot of honest discussion about behaviors in the group and, of course, a willingness to grow and change. The section on group behaviors in Appendix I (pages 129-31) includes a reflection for testing out behaviors in the group, and suggests a variety of uses for this activity. I recommend that every group use it or some such process at least annually.

The skills that the communication theorists term "process skills" are the basis for group dialogue. They need to be reviewed and discussed often, and group members need to assist each other in the process of practicing these skills. A section on process skills is also included in Appendix I (pages 125-28).

There is an abundance of "how to" books and manuals on meeting skills and procedures. A word of caution, however, is appropriate. So much of what is written and taught about meeting skills presumes that the group is following a parliamentary process. Be careful of accepting everything that is suggested. Discuss the appropriateness of the ideas to the shared wisdom model and then use what is applicable and disregard what is not.

LONG-RANGE PLANNING AND GOAL SETTING

I put these two together because I believe that they belong together. A board or council, together with the staff and/or the faculty, should be involved in developing a long-range plan and then, through annual goal setting, in translating the long-range plan to things to be accomplished in any given year of the plan.

The most workable long-range plan would seem to be one that continually updates itself in such a way that during the first year of implementation of a five-year plan the group is already making plans for the sixth year. At any rate, it must be understood that planning is cyclical and, therefore, that evaluation of the implementation always leads to new plans.

When a *council* does long-range planning and goal setting, it needs to provide ways that the total parish can feed ideas and concerns into the process. This planning is done with the staff. When a *board of education* does long-range planning and goal setting, it needs to provide a way that the parent community can feed ideas and concerns into the process. This planning is done with the faculty.

The shared wisdom model calls for a discerned approach to planning and goal setting. The techniques of management by objectives that we have used in the past do not fit the new model too well because they rely too much on the win-lose mentality in determining priorities. It is possible, however, to adjust the management-by-objectives model and redesign it to include the reflecting, sharing of wisdom, and arriving at agreed-upon goals that can be unanimously accepted as the will of the Spirit.

Make no mistake about it, good planning takes time and skill in any model. It may even take more time in the shared wisdom model. An explanation of long-range planning is given in Appendix I (pages 135-38).

Part of the annual goal-setting task is to make an effort to identify those issues that will need to be discerned in the course of any given year so that a calendar can be realistically developed. This calendar of events should also include special times of retreat and reflection, in-service opportunities, and times for Eucharistic and social celebrations.

HEARING FROM THE PUBLICS

Accountability is a word that groups like to use when describing their relationships to their constituencies. But I find that most boards or councils are not too good at spelling out the concept in behaviors that, in fact, cause them to be accountable to those constituencies. For me to be accountable to another person requires (1) that I know what the other expects of me, (2) that the expectation is realistic and based on what it is I am supposed to do or be, (3) that I seek input from the other in terms of how I am to go about my task or responsibility, and (4) that I report back. Translating this in terms of a parish council or board, we find that the council or board must be clear on what the parish expects of it, but the parish must be realistic in those expectations. That realism will come out of an understanding of the role of the council or board and some knowledge of the procedures it follows. Although the council or board is elected to make decisions and set goals, it is not to do so in a vacuum. Input from the parish at large and from appropriate groups within the parish should be sought. But simply asking people for their input is not enough. The decision makers must get back to the people who share their wisdom, their hopes, their fears, and their dreams and let them know what happened or did not happen and why.

There are a number of structures that promote such accountability. I do not think the open meeting is necessarily one of them. In fact, the longer I work with decision-making groups in church, the less kindly I feel toward open meetings, although I have seen some boards and councils use them well and some parish and parent communities respond effectively. Groups that I work with often ask me how they can increase attendance at their open meetings. The question puzzles me. Upon inquiring I am usually told that the people who now come to these meetings tend to be the ones that the board or council wishes would have stayed home! So, why do they want more of them present? All teasing aside, I really am not at all convinced that open meetings accomplish that much for either the board or council or for their constituents.

There are, however, two structures that I think should be built into the responsibilities of boards and councils. They are consultations and open forums. Consultations provide the gathering of wisdom from the group that will be affected by a decision. If, for example, the parish board of education is considering the adoption of a policy that would mandate the involvement of parents in the sacramental preparation of their children, the board members ask themselves that very important question: Who will this affect? The answer is quite clear: the parents of those children preparing to receive the sacraments. So, consultations will need to be planned with those parents. Such meetings serve to allow the board and staff (1) to explain the reasons behind the proposed policy and (2) to hear from parents regarding what they see as the advantages and disadvantages of such an approach as well as any assistance they might need to implement this policy in their own family setting. How often should such a consultation be held? As often as consideration of a policy or a goal will affect a part or all of the constituency. Of course, consultations need to be well planned and well publicized. However, if people choose not to attend, that is their problem, not the board's. Nor should the board take abuse from a parent who chooses not to be present for the consultation and then, after the policy is adopted, complains about it or refuses to cooperate with it. All such situations must be handled with gentle but firm responses and action plans.

The open forum, the second structure to be considered, is an excellent means of both fostering accountability and seeking out the broader wisdom of the parish or parent community. I would like to say a number of things about this process. First of all, how often should an open forum be held? It is often helpful for a board or council to do this on an annual basis, but then again some groups tell me they find this process too involved to do that frequently. They also tell me that people tend to become less enthusiastic and less involved in the process if an open forum is held annually. Maybe a rule of thumb will be helpful: If yours is a parish or school that has many new families moving in or a school to which many young families are bringing their firstborn child each year, it might be crucial that you hold an annual open forum. On the other hand, if yours is a stable parish or school population, such a frequent forum may not be appropriate. You must also consider such things as where you are in the planning process during any given year. If you are just beginning the process of long-range planning, you will certainly want to conduct an open forum that year. Or if you are at the other end of the process, that is, in the fourth or fifth year of the implementation of the plan, you will want to plan an open forum to provide input on evaluation. Each board or council will have to make its own decision about frequency and do what seems most useful for themselves and most honest in terms of relating to their constituencies.

The way an open forum is conducted can make the difference between an effective experience and a disaster! This discussion, by the way, also applies to consultations. I cannot tell you how many times I have been present at an open forum and have watched a well-meaning chairperson stand up before the assembly and self-destruct! The scenario usually begins with warm words of welcome and gratitude and then the stage is set. Smiling graciously at the assembly, the chairperson says, "Now, suppose you tell us what you think about . . ." and the assembly responds! What usually follows is so devastatingly negative that everyone leaves the forum wondering if anything good ever happens in this parish or school or religious education program. And all because the first question was asked incorrectly.

Let me give you the theory as the communication theorists explain it. Most people (the theorists say close to 95 percent) tend to think negatively. They will not think positively unless specifically required to do so. You may find that statistic hard to believe. If you have worked at getting feedback from people, you will probably have no trouble believing it, however! Let me translate the theory into a little scenario. When people hear the question, "Now, suppose you tell us what you think about . . ." 95 percent of them immediately and automatically decode the question and what they hear is, "What don't you like?" And that is exactly what they will tell you because that is what you have asked them! You said, "What do you think . . ." and they think in negatives!

Now, let's suppose that you have one hundred people at your open forum. If you are lucky, the five positive thinkers will come forward. At least ten or fifteen or even twenty others may speak, all making negative comments. By the end of that session the board, the staff, the principal, or the faculty will leave the assembly thinking that for every one person who approves of what is going on, there are three or four who do not. In addition, one hundred people will walk out of that room thinking to themselves, "That's strange. I always thought we had a pretty good thing going for us. I wonder what went wrong."

See what I mean by self-destruction? And leaders do it over and over again without realizing that they are creating the stage for such a scenario.

What can be done to avoid this situation? What can be done to get valid feedback which will, of course, include some negatives but will have balance?

Two things are necessary: (1) the people must be allowed time to reflect on the issues *before* they come to the forum and (2) the right questions must be asked! And what are the right questions? Well, what the board or council really needs to know is what is good, helpful, and positive and what is not. So that is exactly what must be asked for. A reflection sheet can be prepared and copies distributed in advance of the meeting. The copies can be inserted in the bulletin, sent home with the children, or even mailed. The reflection sheet should list the topics to be dealt with at the open forum and then ask three questions about each topic:

1. What do you like about the way we are doing this?
2. What would you change and how would you change it?
3. What would you add and how would you add it?

Each person coming to the forum is asked to prepare from this reflection sheet and to come ready to share his or her wisdom accordingly. It is critical to the process that those persons facilitating the forum ask the questions in the order in which they are listed. It is also imperative that people respond to the total question; in other words, they must not only say what they would change or add but tell how they would do it.

Such an approach does a couple of things that are helpful for all concerned. First of all, it allows people to respond to the positive things that are happening in the parish, diocese, or school. Second, it does not allow for the luxury of complaining without also providing solutions to concerns and problems. This approach will provide any group with valid and constructive information about programs and future directions it may pursue.

EVALUATION

All too many of us connect the term *evaluation* with a pass-fail mentality. It may relate back to our school days when we got report cards and test results that determined if we "made it" or not. This is an unfortunate concept of evaluation because it denies its most important outcome: an opportunity for improvement and professional growth.

Boards and councils have a serious mandate to be about evaluation in all the areas of their responsibilities. This means that the following will require evaluation:

- Internal operations and goals of the council or board
- Goals of the parish or school
- Operational philosophy
- Policies
- Relationships to constituencies
- Effectiveness of committees and commissions
- Agreed-upon goals and objectives as well as job descriptions of administrator(s)

There are, of course, many ways to evaluate. My own experience tells me that the simpler the process is, the better the results will be. Here are some key questions to keep in mind when developing evaluation models and procedures.

- What did we want this goal, program, committee, process, administrator to accomplish?
- Was the end result accomplished?
- If it was, to what degree of effectiveness?
- If it was not, why not?

Once the information has been gathered, the next step is simply to sit down with the person or group involved and discuss how the strengths can be enhanced and the weaknesses lessened.

Sensitivity to the reliability of those doing the evaluating is important, as is timing and frequency. Some things call for annual evaluation while others do not.

Valid evaluation experiences lead people and groups to develop future goals and objectives that will promote growth and improvement. Evaluation should provide the opportunity for the board or council to affirm those being evaluated while challenging them to a renewed commitment to be and to build church!

Focus Questions for Chapter 8

1. Identification of nominees:

How would you prepare the parish? _____

_____

_____

What process would work for you? _____

_____

_____

2. Formation and in-service:

What kinds of formation and in-service does your group need?

_____

_____

3. Group leadership:

What help does your group need? _____

_____

_____

How could you provide that help? _____

_____

_____

4. Agenda planning:

What changes do you need to make? _____

_____

_____

5. Meeting skills:

What help do you need? _____

_____

_____

How could the group improve its meeting skills? _____

_____

_____

_____

6. Long-range planning and goal setting:

How well do you do this now? _____

_____

_____

What skills do you need to learn?_____

_____

_____

What assistance do you need?_____

_____

_____

7. Hearing from the publics:

How well do you do this now? _____

_____

_____

What might improve the level of communication and wisdom sharing within your group?

_____

_____

8. Evaluation:

How do you evaluate your own performance? _____

_____

_____

How are you involved in the evaluation of the administrator(s)?

_____

_____

_____

What needs to change in order to achieve greater effectiveness in your role in the evaluation process?

_____

_____

_____

Moving Toward the New Model

How does a board, council, team, or staff move from the traditional, quasi-business model to a church model of shared decision making? Patiently, carefully, slowly, and prayerfully.

One of the greatest pieces of wisdom of all times is the sage's recommendation: "If it isn't broken, don't fix it!" So what are the signs of brokenness that would indicate the readiness of a council, board, staff, or faculty to consider a new model? I pick them up in the questions that members of a group ask me or each other about their reactions to meetings. For example:

- Why do we fight/argue so much?
- How come I always feel as though I just lost?
- Why do I feel as though it's "us" against "them"?
- Why does it always seem as if the pastor/religious education director/principal is withholding information that we should have?

Administrators ask a different set of questions that point to brokenness, including the following:

- How come I catch myself getting so defensive when I'm asked a question?
- Why do I dread those meetings?
- How come I have the feeling that it's "me" against "them"?
- Why do they always try to get into administrative issues instead of trusting me to do my job?

Many groups in today's church have already moved beyond some of these destructive behaviors and have intuitively realized that "there has to be a better way to do this." Some groups have adopted and adapted various consensus models and have come to approach their tasks in a spirit of prayerful reflection. Their difficulties seem to result from the fact that the new model just "evolved" and the structure is not clear, especially to new members coming into the group. This creates mixed expectations and often results in the breakdown of the model.

Then there are those whose spirituality and understanding of church are calling them beyond an effective management model to a way of truly being and building church through the combined efforts of laity, religious, and clergy. They have begun the slow process of internalizing the call of Vatican II.

Both of these situations indicate a readiness, or at least a need, to consider a shared wisdom model as an option.

So where does a group start? Obviously this book is meant to provide an understanding of the model as well as its many practical implications and applications. The group that has been reading, reflecting, and sharing its wisdom with the focus questions now needs to give serious consideration to the possibility of adopting the shared wisdom model. Most helpful at this stage of the group's development would be a day of reflection. The goal of the day would be to prayerfully discern the future direction for the board, council, or staff. Who directs the day would depend on the group. It might be the pastor or a member of the staff, or an outside facilitator might be identified. The agenda for the day would include a review of the philosophy of shared wisdom and a reflection on that philosophy. (An outline for this review and a reflection activity are given on pages 152-54 of Appendix I.)

To rush this initial step in moving toward the model would be a mistake. People need to buy into the model with as much understanding as possible. There is also the possibility that although most members of the group will really want to move in this direction, a few will be opposed to such a change. It must be possible for those who simply do not feel called to the spirituality or comfortable with the model to remove themselves, gracefully and sincerely, without any stigma attached or any hard feelings or any hint that they are less than what the church is calling them to be.

Once the group has made the decision to adopt the shared wisdom model, some important additional decisions need to be made. It normally takes at least a year for a group to get itself reoriented and to begin to feel at home with the skills and organizational adjustments required by the model. In the meantime, "business as usual" is a reality. It is unlikely that an already operational group will be able to put things on hold for a year!

It is at this point that the greatest commitment of all may be necessary. While continuing its regular monthly meetings, the group

will have to commit itself to additional time during this year of formation. What has worked best with the boards and councils that I have
worked with is to set aside a weekend and three or four Saturdays for
the formation experiences. Some groups have added an extra meeting
each month, and others have tried to extend the regular monthly meetings. The latter does not work at all. The additional monthly meeting
was acceptable but not as satisfactory or effective as the full-day
sessions.

Let me add here that starting with an entirely new group is the
ideal situation. A parish, for example, that has never had a parish council will find that starting with this model is an easier task than redesigning a model that is already in place. That is certainly not to say that
redesigning is impossible. It just takes a little more creativity and
persistence.

The first step to take in the formation process should probably be
a weekend retreat. It is extremely helpful if this takes place away from
the parish or school. I usually recommend a Friday evening and Saturday arrangement. This calls for no small sacrifice and good advance
planning for baby-sitters and substitutes at the parish. But the effort
pays off! The dynamic of being together, sharing, and worshipping is
powerful and unique.

Friday night would be used as a get-acquainted time. If the
members of the group do not know each other very well, some loosely
structured autobiographical sharing would be appropriate. That accomplished, a sheet could be distributed, inviting reflection on three
things:

- Why I agreed to serve on this council/board
- What gifts I bring to the group
- What needs I have if I am to function effectively in the group

It is possible to do the sharing from this sheet that evening. Or it
may seem wise to use the time for more of a social experience and
save the sharing for the next meeting.

Saturday will be a time for reflection, group sharing, and private
and group prayer based on appropriate scriptural references, and will
probably conclude with the celebration of Eucharist. Some of the
materials given in Appendix I would be helpful for this day. Especially
appropriate would be the reflection on the God of the Gathering (page
116) and possibly, also, the one on ministry (page 117).

The goal of the retreat experience will have been accomplished if
the people leave knowing each other at much more than just a casual
level and if they have gained some increased ease with their ability to
share deeply with each other.

The next task will depend on the nature of the group. If this is a
newly organized board or council, at least a day will have to be devoted

to explaining the roles, relationships, and responsibilities involved. Critical to this educational component will be the opportunity to explore at length the distinction between the role of the administration and staff and that of the board or council, keeping clearly in focus the role of the latter as thinkers and planners and of the former as implementers.

There are a number of other areas that the group will need to explore. If the group has a mission statement in place, the members must internalize its implications and remain aware of the statement as they go about their tasks. If the members have not developed a mission statement, the process outlined on pages 132-33 of Appendix I will help them write a statement that reflects their group.

It is often helpful for a group to recognize the different ways in which its members may personally understand and experience church. The summary on page 133 and the reflection activity on page 134 are intended to help clarify an understanding of the various models of church. While the use of this material is critical to any group that is developing a mission statement (it is the first step of the process), I also recommend it as a faith-sharing experience for all groups.

Boards and councils must have a working knowledge of all parish and diocesan policies that will affect their ministry. Such knowledge should be supplied by the pastor, principal, or other appropriate person. Policy books should be given to all members.

If the educational component is all clear and working well, it is time to move on to a day devoted to skill development. This day would concentrate on the process skills, group behaviors, conflict management skills, and the way these interact with a shared wisdom model. The day should include opportunities for group members to practice at least some of the skills presented. It should also provide them with ideas about ways to help each other with this kind of skill development as they continue their regular meetings.

Given these formation and information sessions, the group should now be ready to try its wings and attempt to arrive at a discerned decision. Before doing so, the group should study and discuss the process as it is outlined and explained in Chapter 5 of this book. It is usually wise to have the assistance of a facilitator the first few times the group attempts to use the model. It is critical, however, that the facilitator understands the model and is comfortable with the process and attentive to the work of the Spirit in and through the group.

I am often asked what kinds of decisions are good ones to start with as groups are learning the process and practicing the skills. Identification of group leadership seems to be one effective place to start. A policy decision might also be an appropriate starting place. Simpler than this, perhaps, would be a decision to begin long-range planning or to include a youth minister in next year's budget.

Whatever a group starts with, a number of things should be kept in mind as it actually begins to "work" the model. They include:

- It will take longer than it usually does to arrive at a decision, so the group needs to allow plenty of lead time.
- Reflective prayer must be an integral part of the process.
- With the help of the facilitator, the members of the group should evaluate the process as they move through it.
- The process may not work as smoothly as the members had hoped. They must be patient and keep trying.

Ongoing evaluation is essential to just about anything the group is doing, but it is especially critical to a new model or program. Not just the first year, but *especially* the first year, evaluation needs to be carefully programmed. There are a number of evaluative instruments in Appendix I (pages 145-51). Any evaluation method or tool that the group uses must include the opportunity to express and discuss feelings as well as effectiveness.

Once the model is in place and the group spends the necessary months on formation and in-service, I recommend that the same group be allowed to continue as the board or council for another year unchanged. In other words, there would be no parish election or appointments of new members during year two of the implementation.

When it is appropriate to bring some new members on the council or board, the incumbent members must be sure that the process for identifying nominees is congruent with the shared wisdom model. This is a call to spirituality, a call to ministry. It is the work of the Spirit, not a political campaign. Suggestions for the discernment of potential members can be found in Appendix I (pages 140-43). The group should adjust and adapt them to fit the needs of the parish or diocese, but it must also be aware of allowing the Spirit to call people to this ministry of being and building church.

One last word of caution. This model is not magic! It will not necessarily solve all problems. It is not guaranteed to work. It does not eliminate the human limitations and failures that are such a part of the fabric of our lives and of our church. But it is of the Spirit, and if people are willing to be open to it, they will find themselves growing in the challenge of today's church: to join together as the people of God to be and to build church!

Focus Questions for Chapter 9

1. What needs to be done to initiate a shared wisdom model in your group?

_____

_____

_____

_____

_____

_____

2. How will your group start to learn the process and practice the skills?

_____

_____

_____

_____

_____

_____

3. What kind of a time line does your group want to design?

_____

_____

_____

_____

_____

_____

4. What help does your group need?

_____

_____

_____

_____

_____

_____

On the following pages you will find a great variety of materials and methods that I have used with groups and have found to be supportive of the shared wisdom model. I have tried to provide some "helpful hints for happy using" with the materials, but two comments are in order:

1. Although none of the methods or materials included is all that complicated, to make proper use of them a leader or facilitator needs some experience with group process.

2. It is difficult to design process materials for someone else to use. Therefore, mine should be seen as samples, and anyone using them should feel free to make adjustments that meet his or her style and the needs of the group.

Process experiences are among the most enriching experiences any group will ever have, but they can also be total failures if they are not well planned. Proper planning includes the following:

- Getting the group ready for the experience
- Setting a convenient time and place
- Creating the proper atmosphere
- Having all necessary materials available
- Providing clear directions
- Maintaining an environment that is free from any distractions and interruptions
- Being sensitive to needs and feelings
- Bringing the experience to some degree of closure

PRAYER

I like to describe prayer as "allowing oneself to be available to God." Such availability is crucial to the shared wisdom model because, as I have said, we can be attentive to the God of the Gathering only if we are attentive to the God who lives and speaks and touches within our own beings.

In Chapter 3, I spoke of the importance of a personal prayer life, of processing life on a daily basis. Something of that personal spirituality needs to be fostered and treasured in the group experience as well. Prayer within the context of meetings is an absolute must. But such prayer must be well planned to be effective.

Planning Prayer Experiences

Most groups have the custom of beginning a meeting with a Scripture reading, a formal prayer, or perhaps some petitions. I have often wondered, as I have participated in opening prayers, if such prayers did much more than get all the people mentally into the room. If the opening prayer is not a genuine expression of prayer but merely a way of beginning the meeting, it may be just as helpful simply to have a time of quiet in which to center oneself, to get in touch with all the distractions and concerns that have been a part of the day and attempt to let them go, and to ask the Spirit to be present to oneself and to the group.

What is important is not *when* the group prays but that prayer is made a priority. Therefore, time must be given to its preparation as well as to the actual praying. It may be the spiritual leader who prepares the prayer, or other members in the group may desire the opportunity to do this.

It is my suggestion that such prayer be scripturally based. I therefore offer some Scripture references that might be helpful in planning prayer experiences. All of these have some reference to the presence of the Spirit in our lives or in our assemblies.

Deuteronomy 30:11-14	1 Corinthians 1:21-25
Proverbs 8:1-12	2:3-16
8:32-35	12:4-11
Wisdom 6:12-16	2 Corinthians 1:21-22
Isaiah 50:4-5	Colossians 1:27-29
Romans 5:5	1 John 2:20
8:9	2:27
8:14-16	4:2-3
	4:13

One of the groups that I worked with developed the following prayer that all its members prayed frequently during the months of discerning a community decision. I offer it as an example of the kind of prayer that personalizes where the group is and what it is feeling and needing.

Prayer to the Holy Spirit

Loving God, we come to You seeking Your preference in our lives.

Fill us with Your spirit of quiet listening, faith-filled freedom, and generous response.

Touch our minds and hearts so that we may have eyes to see and ears to hear what You ask of us in our ministry.

Heal us that we may heal each other through Your compassionate love and mercy.

This we ask in the name of Your Son, Jesus, and His Holy Spirit.

Amen.

—Benedictine Sisters
Benet Hill Priory
Colorado Springs

The following two prayer experiences are samples of the kinds of things that can be done when the group takes the time to stay with prayer for a period of time. The first one, "Hearing God's Call," could be done within the context of a regular meeting. It is an effort to touch that God who calls us through our own lived experiences and thus to recognize His call in whatever form it takes. The connection between this and responding to the God of the Gathering is obvious.

The second prayer experience, "A Liturgy of Affirmation," is the kind one might include in a day of reflection. It usually takes at least two hours and often longer, depending on the size of the group. The part called "The Affirmation Experience" is the heart of the prayer. At this time the group gathers in a circle. One member is chosen to be "first" to be affirmed. All the other members of the group take turns speaking to the one being affirmed. Each says something like this: "What I admire most in you is . . ." or "The quality in you that I would like to develop in myself is . . ." The person being affirmed makes no response during this time; but when everyone has finished, he or she responds in whatever way seems appropriate and comfortable. Some people will just say a simple "Thank you!" Others are more articulate and comment on various remarks that have been made. The only thing that is out of order is the denial of something someone has said. The point is to just enjoy being told some good things about yourself!

When everyone has been affirmed, the prayer continues with the petitions. It's a beautiful experience for a group to share. I recommend it highly!

Hearing God's Call

(It would facilitate this experience if everyone had paper and pencil before beginning the call to prayer.)

Call to Prayer
Leader: Lord God, we come together to hear Your Word.
All: Open us to Your Spirit, Your call, Your love.

Scripture Reading
       1 Samuel 3:1-11

Directed Reflection
Leader: Many times in our lives God calls us. Sometimes we don't even hear His call. Other times we hear it but we are not at all sure where the call is coming from or what it means. During this prayer experience we will have a short time to get in touch with God's call in our lives.

Please consider, for a minute or two, some "intersection" in your life, that is, some time when there were two options for you—to go to college or to get a job, to move to this city or to that one or to this parish or another one, to become active in your parish or to be just a "member."

(Pause for a few minutes.)*

Jot down on your paper what "intersection" you want to consider. Now, list the possibilities that were available to you at that intersection and circle the option you chose.

(It would be helpful if you would share your intersection, the possibilities, and the option chosen.)

I now invite you to carry on a dialogue with God. It will probably help you if you write your dialogue. However, if writing gets in the way, don't force it.

In this conversation with God try to get in touch with what He was *saying* to you about your life, what He was *preparing* you for, what He was *teaching* you about yourself. *Ask* Him. *Listen* for His answer. *Discuss* it with Him.

(Allow five to seven minutes for this dialogue.)

I invite you now to turn to the person next to you and share with him or her what you have learned or how you feel about your reflection.

(Allow three to five minutes for this activity. Again, it would be helpful if you would share your own feelings about the reflection before asking the group to do so.)

---

*All instructions given in parentheses are directed to the leader.

Having considered a time in each of our lives when God called us through the circumstances of our lives, let us now listen again to the Scripture passage.

(Reread 1 Samuel 3:1–11.)

And let us pray:

> God, loving Father,
> You call us to Your life,
>   Your love.
>
> You shape our world,
>   our lives.
>
> You care for us,
>   challenge us,
>   guide us,
>   form us.
>
> May we recognize Your call
> and respond to it lovingly,
>   generously,
>   and joyfully!
>
> We ask this through Your Son and the Spirit.
>
> Amen.

A Liturgy of Affirmation

Leader: "But now the Lord who created you says: 'Don't be afraid, for I have ransomed you; I have called you by name; you are mine. When you go through deep waters and great trouble, I will be with you. When you go through rivers of difficulty, you will not drown . . . flames will not consume you. For I am the Lord your God, your savior, the Holy One of Israel. . . . You are precious to me and honored and I love you. Don't be afraid, for I am with you.'"

Isaiah 43:1–5
(The Living Bible)

Let us reflect on this word of the Lord.

The Affirmation Experience

(See page 107 for the procedure of affirming each member of the group by all the others.)

Prayers of Petition

Response: Lord, hear our grateful prayer:

That we may realize the implications of being created by our God,

That we may hear the Lord as He calls us by name,

That we may believe that the Lord loves us, that we are precious to Him and honored by Him,

That our faith may be stronger than our fear,

That we may serve our church with the skill we have each been given and with joy,

That we may value one another and ourselves.

Prayer: Lord, we thank You for the talents present in this group.

We are grateful for our gifts.

We see the reflection of You and Your goodness in ourselves and in one another.

We humbly ask that we may use our gifts wisely and for Your glory.

We ask this through Your Son and the Spirit.

Amen.

Developing Prayer Experiences for Meetings

The following are some helpful hints on preparing group prayer experiences.

Identifying a Theme

Two questions are significant:

1. What is the meeting about?
2. Is this a feast or a special liturgical season?

With regard to the first question, the theme might flow from the fact that the group is meeting for such reasons as the following:

- To make a decision
- To determine leadership
- To solve a problem
- To plan for a special event
- To celebrate
- To evaluate
- To begin a project
- To conclude a project

Or the time of the year may be important:

- Advent
- Christmas
- Lent
- Easter
- Pentecost

Whatever the theme, it should flow out of one or both of these questions; and readings, songs, prayers, and so on, need to reflect the theme.

Developing the Experience

Call to Prayer
> This is often a song or a simple greeting and response.

Scripture Reading
> The reading should be short and should highlight the theme.
> The planner should learn to use a concordance.
> The planner should check out the different translations of the Bible and choose the one that seems most appropriate for the group.

Response to Reading

| A psalm or part of one | Music |
| A song or hymn | Silence |

Prayer

| Petitions | Our Father |
| Spontaneous petitions | A collect |

Closing
>A song or hymn
>A blessing

The Setting

Place
>The prayer may take place in the same location as the meeting or elsewhere.

"Props"
>| | |
>|---|---|
>| Bible | Lighting |
>| Candles | Music |
>| Plants | Copies of the service |
>| Banner | |

Preparation
>Caution readers to be alert to inclusive language.
>Provide materials.
>Explain the prayer service before beginning to pray.

Helps for Planning

A concordance

Different translations of the Bible

The following references:
>Deiss, Lucien. *Biblical Prayers.* Cincinnati: World Library Publications, 1976.
>
>Geissler, Eugene, ed. *The Bible Prayer Book.* Notre Dame: Ave Maria Press, 1981.
>
>Hintz, Debra. *Prayer Services for Parish Meetings.* Mystic, Conn.: Twenty-Third Publications, 1983.
>
>Reutemann, Charles. *Let's Pray: Fifty Services for Praying Communities.* Winona, Minn.: St. Mary's Press, 1975.
>
>Schmidt, Joseph F. *Praying Our Experience.* Winona, Minn.: St. Mary's Press, 1980.

FAITH SHARING AND THEOLOGICAL REFLECTION

People in ministry need to share more than just the ministry. They need to share themselves. To the degree that members of a council, board, staff, or faculty can share more than ideas and concerns, they will begin to build the faith community that is called for in this shared wisdom model. And what are we to share? It is especially important to share our faith lives, our feelings, and our lived experience.

Some people do this very easily and naturally. Others find it quite difficult. But deep down inside each of us is a desire to tell our stories—

stories of pain and failure, joy and success, stories about how God touches and forms us and walks the journey with us. Faith sharing and theological reflection are ways of doing just that.

Often a Scripture passage will serve as the best starter for such sharing. Let us say, for example, that the chosen Gospel reading is the story of the wedding feast at Cana. After the Gospel is proclaimed, the prayer leader might simply say, "Let us reflect on how Jesus takes the 'water' that is our human limitations and weaknesses and turns it into His 'wine.'" It is important that a few minutes of silence be allowed for the reflection. Those who wish to share their thoughts with the group should be invited to do so. This reflection and sharing should not be rushed. Times of silence between sharing are appropriate. And not everyone should be expected to share, at least not at first.

Sometimes it is helpful to prepare some materials in advance on a specific topic, such as the following short reading on discernment and the accompanying reflection activity. If this approach is to be used, the reading and the reflection should be assigned when the agenda is sent out so that the members will come prepared to share. Reflection 1 can be used in different ways. The leader may just want each person to share his or her prayer. But if the group members have had some previous experience with faith sharing, they may choose to deal with the individual questions. This could be done over a number of meetings or during a day of reflection when there would be adequate time to devote to it.

Theological reflection allows the group to take some basic concept and match it to their own lived experience. Reflections 2-5 are given as examples. These, too, need to be assigned well in advance of the meeting if quality sharing is to be expected.

Such experiences serve to bond the group. They also provide each member with insights about the other members. These insights in turn help the members understand why people take the positions they take or have the fears or concerns they have. Such insights also encourage members to be patient and compassionate with one another, and make it possible for them to call one another to new places of growth.

A Prayerful Reflection on the Gift of Discernment*

Both contemplation and discernment are experiences of the indwelling God, gifts that represent growth in the life of the Spirit. Contemplation is the experience of God *in Himself.* Discernment is the experience of God *in a given human situation.* Discernment asks us to be contemplative in our actions and in our choices. Discernment calls us to find that same God in community that we discover in our prayer.

Discernment is spirituality in the concrete: the awareness of the Spirit acting within us as we gather to be and to build church. It is experiencing with understanding and commitment the presence and guidance of God in one's whole life. Discernment is a life work!

Discernment is founded on three basic relationships: to self, to God, and to others. The relationship to self is primarily based on the recognition of brokenness; to God, the attitude of trust; and to others, a willingness to dialogue.

Discernment demands an attitude of holy indifference: a total openness to God, a freedom, an ability to let go and to move in whatever direction God calls.

How does one test the validity of a discerned choice? A discerned life? If the Lord is present and acting, the signs will be there: a joy in suffering, peace even in persecution.

Discernment cannot be successfully carried out if it is only an occasional act that is foreign to one's usual life patterns. We discern as well as we live and we live as well as we discern!

The person in tune with the Spirit is a free and loving human being, one who no longer depends on self-gratification, success, popularity, or winning in order to be happy. This person's strength comes from deep within, where the Spirit dwells. Such a life shows a person becoming more and more human, more deeply joyful and more loving.

> As for Mary, she treasured all these things and pondered them in her heart.
>
> *Luke 2:19*

Mary's life was an effort to hear, to understand, to ponder, to surrender, to search, to keep all that happened and all that was said in the depths of her heart.

We, like Mary, are discerning as long as we search and surrender!

---

*Summarized from *Silent Presence: Discernment As Process and Problem* by Ernest Larkin (Denville, N.J.: Dimension Books, 1981).

REFLECTION 1
The Gift of Discernment

1. Identify a contemplative experience you have had, that is, an experience of God *in Himself.*

2. Identify a discernment experience you have had, that is, an experience of God in a *human situation.*

3. When have you found God in your experience of church?

4. What is your experience of your own brokenness?

5. What is your experience of trusting God?

6. What is your experience of genuine dialogue in the parish?

7. What is your experience of holy indifference in your own life?

8. How free are you? _____

9. How loving are you? _____

10. How joyful are you? _____

Complete this prayer in words that have meaning for you. Make it as short or as long as you need it to be. You may want to pray it frequently.

Father, You give us Your Spirit to be the presence of Your
Son Jesus in our lives and in this parish. Help me to . . .

_____

_____

_____

_____

_____

_____

_____

REFLECTION 2
The God of the Gathering

1. What is your experience of gathering in—

your family? _____

_____

your parish? _____

_____

the world? _____

_____

2. What is your experience of bondedness in—

your family? _____

_____

your parish? _____

_____

the world? _____

_____

3. What is your experience of fragmentation in—

your family? _____

_____

your parish? _____

_____

the world? _____

_____

4. What is your experience of healing in—

your family? _____

_____

your parish? _____

_____

the world? _____

_____

REFLECTION 3
Ministry

1. How are you nourished and strengthened as a result of your experience of church?

_____

_____

_____

_____

_____

2. What prevents you from being nourished and strengthened by church?

_____

_____

_____

_____

3. How do you nourish and strengthen others in your experience of ministry?

_____

_____

_____

_____

_____

4. What prompts you to provide this ministry?

_____

_____

_____

_____

5. What prevents you from providing this ministry?

_____

_____

_____

_____

REFLECTION 4
The Gift of the Spirit

The Spirit is given to each of us for the good of all of us.
1 Corinthians 12:7

1. What is your experience of the Spirit being given to you in your own life?

_____

_____

_____

_____

_____

_____

2. What is your experience of the Spirit being given to you as a member of the council, board, or staff?

_____

_____

_____

_____

_____

_____

3. How do you share this gift with others in your life?

_____

_____

_____

_____

_____

4. How do you share this gift with others on the council, board, or staff?

_____

_____

_____

_____

_____

REFLECTION 5
The Renewing Church

Before you do this reflection, reread the poem "In Search of a Round Table" on pages 31-33.

1. What is your experience of "round tabledness" in relation to—

   church leadership? _____

   _____

   _____

   the laity? _____

   _____

   _____

2. What is your experience of "narrowlong ministers" in relation to—

   church leadership? _____

   _____

   _____

   the laity? _____

   _____

   _____

3. What is your experience of "narrowlong guests" in relation to—

   church leadership? _____

   _____

   _____

   the laity? _____

   _____

   _____

4. In your experience, what promotes or fosters "round tabledness" in a church board or council?

   _____

   _____

   _____

   _____

   _____

GIFTS, NEEDS, AND EXPECTATIONS

In the book *The Parish in Community and Ministry,* Evelyn Eaton Whitehead makes the following observation:

> Each of us carries, perhaps only implicitly, our own defini-
> tions or descriptions of an active parishioner, a good priest, a suc-
> cessful parish council, a dedicated religious, a good parish team.
> These descriptions function as ideal types, providing the criteria
> against which we will evaluate the actual parishioners, priests, par-
> ish councils, religious men and women, and parish teams whom
> we experience. Complications can arise when persons set about to
> live together, to work together, to share their experience of faith,
> each with slightly differing images and ideals of sharing, of cooper-
> ation, of authority, of leadership. The diversity in itself is not the
> problem. . . . Diversity—within certain wide margins—is a potential
> resource for the community. The problem, often, is that these dif-
> ferences are not acknowledged and appreciated. (1)

How we perceive one another as members of a parish council or a school board, or any group that is called to minister within an organizational structure, is critical to the functioning of the group as well as to the productivity, satisfaction, and well-being of each member. But it is more than just expressing how we see one another in our roles. A number of insights need to be shared, including:

- The gifts that each member of the group brings to the task and to the commitment
- The needs that each member has if he or she is to function well
- The expectations each member has of all the others
- The acknowledgment of each member of what the others can expect of him or her

Trust is critical to the shared wisdom model. Trust is built on knowledge and respect. The kind of personal sharing involved in talking about gifts and needs and expectations is an excellent first step for building such trust.

One word of caution as the group enters into this process. The wisdom that people will be sharing comes from their own lived experience. There is no way anyone can deny me *my* lived experience! Yet, it is not uncommon to find someone in a group who, when another shares an experience, will say, "Oh, you don't need to feel that way about that!" The fact remains, however, that the person does feel that way, and to deny the validity of such a feeling is to deny a basic freedom of that person to be. Such comments on the part of well-meaning people who do not want another to suffer or feel inadequate can be extremely destructive and need to be avoided.

This sharing experience is not a time for debate, for argument, or even for discussion. It is a time to listen, to respect, and to treasure the revelations people are making about their feelings and needs.

The information provided in this section can be given to the members of a group for their reflection and discussion before the process begins; or it can be presented by a facilitator, elaborated upon to whatever degree seems appropriate, and discussed by the group as necessary.

It seems unlikely that Reflections 6-8 could be handled in a single session unless perhaps it is a day-long experience. What is more likely is that the reflections on gifts and needs would be done at one session and the reflection on expectations at another time.

People could be asked to fill out the reflections in advance and come ready to share their thoughts, or completing the activities could be part of the time together.

It is, of course, absolutely necessary that the information written on these pages be shared with the total group that will be working together. Otherwise the purpose of the exercise will not be accomplished.

REFLECTION 6
Gifts

Consider your gifts. These gifts will include experiences you have had as well as interests, knowledge, and things you do well, enjoy doing, are successful at doing. Consider also your motivation for joining the group and your desire to contribute to its success.

Now, list all the gifts you bring to the group.

REFLECTION 7
Needs

Consider your needs. These needs will flow from your experiences in other groups, the skills or knowledge you may feel that you lack, and your fears about your status in the group.

Now, list all the needs that you bring to this group, and tell how other members of the group may be able to respond to your needs.

_____

_____

_____

_____

_____

_____

_____

_____

_____

_____

_____

_____

_____

_____

_____

_____

_____

_____

_____

_____

_____

_____

_____

_____

REFLECTION 8
Expectations

Your expectations of people in various roles will flow out of your experience of people who have filled these roles to your personal satisfaction—or have failed to! With this in mind, reflect on the following and write your responses.

1. I expect the (pastor, principal, religious education coordinator, chairperson, members of the group) to:

_____

_____

_____

_____

_____

_____

_____

_____

_____

_____

2. The (pastor, principal, religious education coordinator, chairperson, members of the group) can expect me to:

_____

_____

_____

_____

_____

_____

_____

_____

_____

_____

_____

THE PROCESS SKILLS

These are meeting skills that support the shared wisdom model and allow the wisdom of the group to surface. When a group develops competency in these skills, the responsibility for decision making and for the success of the meeting falls equally on every participant.

Task Skills

Task skills refer to behaviors that are concerned with the group getting its job done. They are:

- *Initiating*—Bringing new ideas, questions, and suggestions to the attention of the group. Clarity is critical to the skill of initiating.
- *Seeking information*—Requesting facts, ideas, opinions, feelings. Sincerity in seeking others' wisdom is necessary.
- *Giving information*—Offering facts, information, concerns, suggestions. Each member of the group needs to recognize his or her obligation to share wisdom.
- *Clarifying*—Interpreting information and ideas, defining terms, clearing up confusion. Clarifying saves much wasted time.
- *Summarizing*—Pulling together related ideas, restating what has been discussed. This allows the group to move on to the next step.
- *Tracking the agenda*—Bringing the group or an individual back on target, keeping the group focused, confronting topic jumpers. Practicing this skill is often an uncomfortable but necessary task.
- *Consensus testing*—Doing a "whip-around," a quick survey of each member, to see if the group is near a decision, testing a possible conclusion, checking that all the wisdom has surfaced. This is a most useful skill, especially for the chairperson or leader.

Maintenance Skills

These skills are important to the morale of the group. By developing these skills, group members maintain good and harmonious working relationships and create an atmosphere that enables each member to contribute maximally. These skills include:

- *Gatekeeping*—Controlling the channels of communication by (1) opening gates (helping others get into the discussion) and (2) closing gates (providing equal time for all)
- *Encouraging*—Supporting, being friendly, showing interest in the discussion, indicating an attitude of respect for others' wisdom
- *Negotiating*—Considering compromise, identifying what is agreed upon as well as what is in conflict, modifying in the interest of the group, trusting the wisdom of the group

- *Standard testing and setting*—Testing group satisfaction with norms and procedures, offering alternatives for consideration
- *Expressing feelings*—Verbalizing feelings, trusting the validity of personal feelings
- *Tracking the discussion*—Bringing the group back to a point that has been lost or ignored, getting the group going again

Decision-Making Skills

Groups are making decisions all the time. They must understand how decisions are being made and judge the appropriateness of the process. Inappropriate decision-making techniques are described below. In each case someone in the group needs to name what has happened and ask that all members of the group be allowed to share wisdom and participate in the decision.

1. *The plop* occurs when the group makes a decision by ignoring the contribution and the person making the contribution. This is always a negative way of making a decision. The group needs to deal with lost wisdom.

2. *The self-authorized decision* happens when someone announces a decision and carries it out without checking with the group. If the group allows this to happen, the self-authorized decision becomes the group's decision.

3. *The handclasp* happens when one member of the group supports another's suggestion and the two proceed to make a decision without checking it out with the group. If the group allows this to happen, the decision of the two members becomes the group's decision.

4. *A minority decision* occurs when a subgroup railroads a decision through.

5. *A majority decision* is made when a majority is allowed to push through a decision over the objections of the minority. Because it is a win-lose situation, this is an inappropriate way to arrive at decisions in a shared wisdom model.

The group needs to agree in advance that all decisions will be consensus decisions. Only then will the group be able to arrive at decisions that can be lived with gracefully by all of its members.

Those involved in a shared wisdom model will need to learn these process skills, practice them, and evaluate their own performance as well as the group's growth and faithfulness to these skills. Reflections 9 and 10 are provided to guide groups in testing their understanding and skill development.

REFLECTION 9
Understanding the Process Skills

1. What are the implications of the process skills for you, that is, what behavior of yours needs to be changed?

_____

_____

_____

_____

2. What are the implications of the process skills for the group, that is, what changes need to be made in the behavior of the group?

_____

_____

_____

_____

3. What are your hopes about the group's willingness or ability to change?

_____

_____

_____

_____

4. What are your fears and concerns about the group's willingness or ability to change?

_____

_____

_____

_____

5. What recommendations would you make to yourself and to the group about how you and the other members can use the process skills?

_____

_____

_____

_____

REFLECTION 10
Developing the Process Skills

1. List the skills that you feel you practice rather consistently.

   Task skills: _____

   _____

   Maintenance skills: _____

   _____

   Decision-making skills: _____

   _____

2. List the skills that you feel you have not given much thought to, but would be willing to try.

   Task skills: _____

   _____

   Maintenance skills: _____

   _____

   Decision-making skills: _____

   _____

3. List the skills that you feel you need to develop.

   Task skills: _____

   _____

   Maintenance skills: _____

   _____

   Decision-making skills: _____

   _____

4. What could you do to develop some of the skills you feel you now lack?

   _____

5. What could others in the group do to help you in your efforts?

   _____

6. How do you think you might be able to help others in the group improve their skills?

   _____

   _____

BEHAVIORS:
The "Real World" of Group Process

As the members of any group work together they will enable one another, neutralize one another, or destroy one another. Very few set out to accomplish the latter. Most want to be enablers of one another. Many are, at best, neutralizers, without even realizing it.

Reflection 11 is designed to help group members recognize attitudes and behavior, own them, share them, and then move on to improve them. All items on the reflection are meant to be self-explanatory, but a word about what I call "filters" might be helpful.

It is my experience that as members of a group we often come to a group situation having placed certain filters over people that make it impossible for us to really hear their wisdom. Like all filters, these mental and emotional filters block something out.

An indicator that such a filter is in operation is a comment such as, "Well of course you will take that position, Father. You're a priest." Or "That's what you always say, Susan. You have a real thing about church envelopes!" These kinds of comments usually indicate that the speaker has placed a filter over Father and Susan and can hear what they are saying only through the screen of that filter. Father may be saying something that has no direct relationship to his priesthood and Susan may even have begun to change her position, but the speaker is not open to any wisdom that has been filtered through "priest" and "a real thing about church envelopes." The filter gets in the way because it limits the amount of information that can get through.

One of the things that I have found helpful in asking people to examine their possible filters is to suggest that they take a good look at something that really annoys them in one person but that they hardly seem to notice in another. This may lead them to discover that they have filtered the first person.

Reflection 11 can be used in a variety of ways. It may be used as a private reflection and a kind of personal examination. Or, it may be seen as a point of departure to enable the group to discuss behaviors in a general kind of way. If the trust level in the group is healthy and the members are fairly comfortable with personal sharing, they may be willing to talk about how they rated themselves and what need for change they recognize. It is also helpful, then, to discuss ways to support and affirm change. If such openness is not appropriate, just sharing the prayers might be insightful.

REFLECTION 11
Group Behaviors

Reflect prayerfully on your own behavior and attitudes as you interrelate with the members of your group.

1. Attentive Listening

How do I listen? (Check those that apply.)

_____ Do I listen in order to judge?

_____ To refute?

_____ To find a place to break into the discussion?

_____ To hear?

Do I listen attentively? _____

Do I have rather consistent filters for certain people? _____

If so, can I identify those filters and explain why I have them? _____

2. Controlling Behaviors

How do I control group behavior? (Check those that apply.)

_____ Do I control it by my silence?

_____ My tears?

_____ My explosions?

_____ My withdrawal?

_____ Other? _____

3. Letting Go

What indicators do I have of my faith in the God of this Gathering?

_____

_____

_____

_____

_____

What indicators do I have that at times I play the messiah?

_____

_____

_____

_____

4. Allowing Consensus to Happen

What do I do to allow the group to arrive at consensus decisions?

_____

_____

_____

_____

_____

_____

_____

_____

What do I do that prevents or delays the group in its efforts to reach consensus?

_____

_____

_____

_____

_____

_____

_____

_____

Lord, God of this Gathering, I pray . . .

_____

_____

_____

_____

_____

_____

_____

_____

_____

_____

WRITING A MISSION STATEMENT

A statement of mission is a broad statement that expresses the reason or purpose for the existence of a group. It unifies, motivates, and clarifies. It answers the questions:
Who are we called to be?
Why do we exist?
What should we be about?

The twelve steps in helping a group develop a mission statement are as follows:

1. Present Avery Dulles's *Models of the Church* (see summary on page 133). Then have the group complete Reflection 12 (page 134) and share their reflection.

2. Ask the group members to reflect on how they would complete these sentences:
I feel called to . . .
I bring to this group . . .
I need from this group . . .

3. Have the members share the wisdom from their reflection.

4. Ask the members to reflect on how they would answer these questions:
Who are we called to be?
Why do we exist?
What should we be about?

5. Have the members share the wisdom from their reflection.

6. Begin to develop a preliminary statement in small groups. Have the groups compare their statements. Then compile the statements, identifying both what is common and what is unique.

7. Assess the draft statement by having the group discuss the following questions:
Does the draft statement reflect Scripture?
Does it reflect the history of the church?
Is it consistent with our lived experience?
Does it give us a strong sense of identity?
Does it foster Catholic values?
Does it challenge us to worship and pray?
Does it call us to respond to the needs of others?

8. Revise the draft statement in light of the group discussion.

9. Test for consensus (repeat steps 8 and 9 as needed).

10. Test the statement out on the larger parish community.

11. Write the final statement.

12. Publish and celebrate!

Models of the Church

This very brief summary of Avery Dulles's book *Models of the Church* (New York: Doubleday, 1978) is offered here as a guide for reflection on the various models. Before this would be helpful to any group, it would be necessary that a presentation or a review of the models be given by someone who is familiar with them as Dulles presents them in his book. After such a presentation this summary and Reflection 12 would be used by the group members to prepare for a faith-sharing experience.

The Church As Institution
Structure . . . visible . . . approved doctrines . . . official teaching . . . salvation through teaching, preaching, and sacraments

The Church As Community
Interpersonal community in Christ . . . reconciling grace of Jesus . . . early church tradition

The Church As Sacrament
People of God . . . liturgy . . . living symbols of Jesus to one another and to the world

The Church As Herald
Proclaim the Word of God . . . church happens where Word is proclaimed . . . Scripture

The Church As Servant
Mission . . . values of Jesus: freedom, justice, peace, charity, compassion, reconciliation . . . reaches beyond itself

The Church As Disciple
Called . . . intimacy . . . sent to preach, to cast out evil, to heal . . . commitment . . . mission . . . Scripture

REFLECTION 12
Models of the Church

Describe your experience of and your feelings about each model of church listed below.

1. The church as institution _____

_____

_____

_____

2. The church as community _____

_____

_____

_____

3. The church as sacrament _____

_____

_____

_____

4. The church as herald _____

_____

_____

_____

_____

5. The church as servant _____

_____

_____

_____

_____

6. The church as disciple _____

_____

_____

_____

_____

LONG-RANGE PLANNING

This overview is meant as a presentation of planning in a shared wisdom model. As such, it repeats much of the theology and philosophy already covered in previous pages. This process is easily adaptable to diocesan and religious community models.

Why Plan?

To say that we can control the future is somewhat presumptuous. To allow the future to control us is less than brilliant! And so we plan.

We accept in faith a loving God who cares about us and for us while we also respect the gifts and talents and wisdom He has given us to take hold of our corporate and individual destinies.

In their book *People in Systems,* Gerard Egan and Michael Cowan say:

> An effectively designed and operating system has clear, operational, behavioral goals that are adequate translations of the mission of the system. (2)

It is just such basic goals that a planning process is designed to identify for the system we call church, be that parish, school, diocese, or community.

Attitudinal Preparation

Some basic stances are necessary if the planning process is to be an experience of church and a helpful tool to move toward the future as a believing community. They are:
• The concept of shared wisdom
• A commitment to shared responsibility
• An understanding of shared decision making in a church model

The philosophy of shared wisdom flows from a very simple belief that when Jesus tells us something, He means for us to believe Him. In the Gospel stories, Jesus promises us, "Whenever you gather together, I am with you." He is telling us that when we come together to break and share bread, He is present. When we come together to pray, He is present. When we come together to nourish and to strengthen church, He is present. From this promise we can come to understand what is meant when we are told in the Scriptures that Jesus is always present through His Spirit: "My Spirit is with you always." We can trust, therefore, that as we come together to plan, the Spirit will be with each of us for the good of all of us. Or, to put it another way, each person in the group is given a different piece of the wisdom! No one person has it all, for no one person can ever contain the total wisdom of the Spirit; nor do we have the same wisdom, for we are given different pieces. The challenge of any group process is to get all the pieces out so as to come as close as possible to the total wisdom the Spirit has to give this group at this time.

There are three important implications of this philosophy:

1. If we each have a piece of the wisdom, we each have a responsibility to share our piece.
2. If we each have a piece, we must listen to all the other pieces.
3. Each member of the group is responsible for helping to create a climate in which wisdom can be both shared and heard.

Shared responsibility implies the acceptance of the philosophy of shared wisdom. It means that each person will do his or her homework all along the way so that personal wisdom will be thought and prayed through, shared and listened to. It also means a genuine effort to hear one another's wisdom, to allow it to open us up to new ways of thinking and seeing and understanding. It means taking a personal responsibility for the process: preparing for meetings, attending meetings, sharing and listening to wisdom, and cooperating all along the way.

To share decisions in a church model is to take the time and make the effort to do the listening, the praying, the sharing that is called for to reach a consensus decision, to let go of the need to win, to allow the Spirit to happen!

The Basic Planning Process

The planning process described here is a seven-step program. The steps are:

1. Developing the statement of mission or focus
2. Assessing the present situation
3. Exploring future inventions
4. Analyzing the data
5. Testing the analysis
6. Setting goals and objectives and determining priorities
7. Implementing and evaluating the goals and objectives

Who Is Involved?

There are four levels of involvement in the planning process:

1. *The parish council or board of education* makes the decision to do long-range planning.
2. *The total parish or school community* is given opportunities to share wisdom at each step of the process and to assume ownership of the mission or focus, the assessment, the analysis, and the goals.

3. *A planning coordinator and a planning commission* are chosen by the parish council or board of education.

4. *Task forces* are identified by the planning commission to do the assessment and the initial analysis in the areas of liturgy, education, pastoral care, peace and justice, administration, and stewardship.

The process is designed with a facilitator in mind. The facilitator would—
- explain the planning process to the parish or school community,
- be responsible for the attitudinal preparation,
- train the planning commission,
- assist the planning commission with design and strategies,
- facilitate general meetings that deal with owning the data, doing the analysis, making assumptions about the future, setting priorities.

Role of the Planning Commission

The planning commission should consist of not less than five and not more than ten members. Its responsibilities include the following:
- Accepting training and formation for the task
- Planning a calendar of events
- Conducting general meetings
- Identifying, training, and assisting the task forces
- Helping in the development of instruments and methods
- Translating the data into goals and objectives
- Testing the proposed goals
- Presenting the goals and objectives
- Recommending time lines and evaluation procedures

Role of the Parish Council

It is possible that some members of the parish council or board may also be on the planning commission, but as members of the council or board they have the following responsibilities:
- Mandating the planning process
- Appointing the commission and coordinator
- Receiving monthly progress reports
- Implementing the process
- Evaluating the process

What Happens at Each Step?

1. In developing the statement of mission or focus, the members of the parish or school community reach agreement on—
- who they are called to be,
- why they exist,

- what they should be about in the light of church, society, and their lived experience.

2. In making their assessment, the task forces collect data on what the group has accomplished and is accomplishing right now.

3. In exploring future inventions the total parish or school community is asked to consider what society, the church, and their parish or school will look like in twenty years.

4. An analysis of the data is done in part by the task forces and the planning commission but also by as many members of the parish or school community as want to be involved. The data are reported to the group by the task forces, and then the group is asked to reflect on the data in the light of the mission statement and the future inventions. The group is also asked to identify—
   - the strengths of the parish/school,
   - the immediate concerns of the parish/school, and
   - the long-range concerns of the parish/school.

5. It is then the responsibility of the planning commission to translate the data into proposed goals. The commission drafts the goals and then spends as much time as is needed (usually two to three months) meeting with organizations, staff people, small groups, and so on, to test out their proposals. At the end of this step the commission prepares its final goals recommendation.

6. It is then the responsibility of the planning commission to present the goals to the parish or school community and to develop a process that will enable the people to reach a consensus and to recommend priorities. It is also important at this point in the process to determine and clarify methods of communication and accountability during the four or five years of implementation.

7. It then becomes the responsibility of the parish council or board to implement and evaluate the long-range goals and objectives.

SOME HELPFUL HINTS FOR POLICY MAKING

- *A policy is a guide for discretionary action.* It is narrow enough to give clear guidance but broad enough to leave room for the discretion of the one who is to implement it.
- *Policy making is the board's/council's responsibility.* A policy tells the administrator *what* to do without ever telling him or her *how* to do it. Policy making is the most important responsibility the board/council has.

- *A regulation is the specification of a policy.* It tells what is to be done to implement the policy. Regulations may be rules or programs.
- *Regulations are determined by the administrator.* The administrator makes these decisions with whatever assistance may be called for by the nature of the task. They are called, therefore, administrative regulations.
- *Policy recommendations are most often generated by the administrator.* While other members of the board/council may recommend policy, the very nature of the administrator's role places him or her in the most likely position to know the needs and therefore to recommend the policies.
- *A procedure for policy development is essential.* The procedure should include the following steps:
  1. Initiation
     a. Prepare a briefing paper.
     b. Add an agenda item for first meeting.
  2. First meeting
     a. Clarify policy recommendation.
     b. Accept the need to deal with the policy recommendation.
     c. Make consultation decisions.
  3. Consultations and data gathering
  4. Reports as needed
  5. Decision making
     a. Analyze results of consultations.
     b. Share wisdom.
     c. Reflect on shared wisdom.
     d. Make appropriate adjustments.
     e. Reach consensus.
- *Policy ideas need to be tested.* Whenever a policy is being considered, it is essential that those to be affected by the policy have a chance to share their wisdom with the policy makers.
- *Policy language is a common language.* It should be nontechnical and easily understood by all publics. A policy that needs interpretation is a poorly written policy. The best policies are usually only a sentence or two in length.
- *Policies are working guides for day-to-day administration.* They must work! Therefore they need to be evaluated regularly, perhaps every three or four years. This can best be done by an ad hoc committee that includes the administrator. Policies that are not working well need to be changed and adjusted.
- *The administrator is accountable to the board/council for the implementation of policy.* While the policy makers do not tell the administrator how to implement policy, it is the responsibility of the

administrator to demonstrate that, in fact, implementation has taken place.

IDENTIFYING MEMBERSHIP

As I have said elsewhere, it seems wise to allow people to make choices for the kingdom, choices for ministry. But such choices must be made realistically. To allow this to happen, people must be able to look at the model, at their own skills, gifts, needs, and motivations, and at the needs of the parish, school, or diocese they seek to serve. The process for doing this is explained on pages 79-81. Reflections 13, 14, and 15 could be used during the process to help the people focus on their spirituality, personal giftedness, and adaptability to the model. At the conclusion of such a discerning experience, each person who feels called to be considered for membership on the council, board, or senate would be encouraged to submit a self-nominating form like the one on page 81. These nominating forms would be processed by the staff and used as a basis for the private session that would be scheduled with each person to test the discernment.

REFLECTION 13
Spirituality

"I call you friends. . . . You did not choose me, no, I chose you; and I commissioned you to go out and to bear fruit."

John 15:15–16

1. Are you willing to devote yourself to the process of spiritual growth, to spending quality time each day with the God who lives life with you?

   When? _____

   Where? _____

   How? _____

2. Are you willing to seek and hear and respect the God of this Gathering in—

   the pastor? _____

   the staff? _____

   other parishioners? _____

3. What would be difficult for you in making a commitment to spiritual growth?

   _____

   _____

   _____

   _____

4. What kind of help and support would you need to continue your spiritual journey?

   _____

   _____

   _____

   _____

5. How would you get that help and support?

   _____

   _____

   _____

   _____

REFLECTION 14
Personal Giftedness

The Spirit is given to each of us for the good of all of us.
1 Corinthians 12:7

1. What gifts would you bring to the group?

_____

_____

_____

_____

_____

_____

_____

_____

2. What limitations would you bring?

_____

_____

_____

_____

_____

_____

_____

3. What help would you need to be able to freely share your piece of the wisdom?

_____

_____

_____

_____

_____

_____

_____

REFLECTION 15
Discerning the Call to Membership

It is the Spirit who gives a different gift to each person as he chooses.
1 Corinthians 12:11

For each of these questions try to give an example.

1. How comfortable are you when speaking and expressing yourself in a group setting?

_____

_____

_____

2. How well do you listen?

_____

_____

_____

3. How strong is your need—

to control? _____

_____

_____

to be correct? _____

_____

_____

to prove your point? _____

_____

_____

4. What is your lived experience of "letting go"?

_____

_____

_____

5. Why do you want to be part of this group?

_____

_____

_____

EVALUATION

Productive councils and boards do not just happen. Staffs and faculties that work well together are not just happy accidents. They work at it! They devote time to spiritual and professional development. And they do regular and effective evaluation.

Evaluation is a tool for growth. To be effective it must be based on agreed-upon expectations and goals. The most effective evaluation is an individual's self-evaluation that is then shared with the leader or group to whom the person is accountable.

What should be evaluated?

- The operational validity of the shared wisdom model
- The operational validity of the mission statement
- The spiritual growth of the group
- The effectiveness of policy and program
- The performance of the administrator(s)

Reflections 16-21 provide some simple evaluation tools. Keep in mind that evaluation usually needs to be an annual experience. It should result in realistic goals that will improve the performance of both the individual and the group.

Note that Reflections 16 and 17 are most useful when working with a group that has already accepted the shared wisdom model and has some operational experience of it.

REFLECTION 16
Evaluation of the Operational Validity
of the Philosophy of Shared Wisdom

Describe your perception of your ability and the group's ability to do each of the following.

1. To experience the presence of the Spirit
   My ability _____

   _____

   The group's ability _____

   _____

2. To hear and share wisdom
   My ability _____

   _____

   _____

   The group's ability _____

   _____

   _____

3. To let go
   My ability _____

   _____

   The group's ability _____

   _____

4. To accept spiritual leadership
   My ability _____

   _____

   The group's ability _____

   _____

5. To take time for prayerful reflection
   My ability _____

   _____

   The group's ability _____

   _____

REFLECTION 17
Evaluation of Group Problem Solving
and Decision Making

Considering the philosophy of shared wisdom, your own behaviors and expectations, and the behaviors and expectations of others in the group, what norms for group problem solving and decision making do you think the group should consider?

_____

_____

_____

_____

_____

_____

_____

_____

_____

_____

_____

_____

_____

_____

_____

_____

_____

_____

_____

_____

_____

_____

_____

REFLECTION 18
Evaluation of a Mission Statement

Complete the following numbered sentences by filling in the major points of your mission statement. For each point you list, describe your lived experience of the call and explain how the group responds to the call, in terms of your personal perceptions. If the group has failed to respond to any call, give the reason.

1. We are called to _____

_____

My lived experience of the call _____

_____

_____

How the group responds _____

_____

_____

2. We are called to _____

_____

My lived experience of the call _____

_____

_____

How the group responds _____

_____

_____

3. We are called to _____

_____

My lived experience of the call _____

_____

_____

How the group responds _____

_____

_____

(Continued on next page)

4. We are called to_____

_____

My lived experience of the call _____

_____

How the group responds _____

_____

5. We are called to_____

My lived experience of the call _____

_____

How the group responds _____

_____

6. We are called to_____

My lived experience of the call _____

_____

_____

How the group responds _____

_____

_____

Share your perceptions in the group. If what is happening in the parish matches what the mission statement is calling the group to be about, the statement is probably valid.

It is possible that the statement is valid but that there are other problems keeping the group from implementing it. Further study of the group's responses should help determine if this is the case and should give some clues about dealing with the problems.

REFLECTION 19
Evaluation of Group Spirituality

We are called to nourish and strengthen church through our ministry. To do this we must also *be* church. This call requires a personal and group spirituality that constantly deepens our relationship with God.

1. In your perception, what are your group's strengths in—

group prayer? _____

_____

prayerful reflection during meetings? _____

_____

Eucharistic celebrations? _____

_____

social celebrations? _____

_____

2. In your perception, what are your group's limitations in—

group prayer? _____

_____

prayerful reflection during meetings? _____

_____

Eucharistic celebrations? _____

_____

social celebrations? _____

_____

3. What are your recommendations to the group? _____

_____

_____

_____

_____

_____

_____

_____

REFLECTION 20
Evaluation of Policy or Program

1. Describe the policy (or program).

_____

_____

_____

_____

2. What is the goal of this policy (program)?

_____

_____

_____

_____

3. How has this policy (program) fulfilled the goal?

_____

_____

_____

_____

4. How has it failed to fulfill the goal?

_____

_____

_____

_____

5. What is your recommendation? (Check one and on the lines below explain your choice.)

_____ This policy (program) should be terminated because:

_____ This policy (program) should be continued because:

_____ This policy (program) should be adjusted to include the following changes:

_____

_____

_____

_____

REFLECTION 21
Personal Evaluation

1. Considering your role and responsibilities in your parish (school), what do you perceive your strengths and limitations to be?

Strengths _____

_____

_____

_____

_____

_____

_____

_____

Limitations _____

_____

_____

_____

_____

_____

_____

_____

2. Based on your strengths and limitations, what goals do you propose for yourself for the coming year?

_____

_____

_____

_____

_____

_____

_____

THE PHILOSOPHY OF SHARED WISDOM

The shared wisdom model offers a very different approach to decision making. Most people involved with boards or councils will come from a background in which a parliamentary model is used. It is my experience that a church group can easily slip back into the win-lose attitude that dominates the parliamentary model, and can get so caught up in the tasks and the demands that it fails to set aside time for reflective prayer and loses attentiveness to the Spirit.

Regular review of and reflection on the shared wisdom model is critical to the performance of any church group. This section contains an outline of the model as it is presented in this book. The outline has multiple uses. One is to serve as a review, to be used with Reflection 22. It could serve the need of both the individuals involved and the total board or council to reflect on and discuss faithfulness and commitment.

The following outline also serves as a guide for a presentation of the shared wisdom model. If a board or council has adopted this model, it is important that its constituent groups be exposed to the philosophy and theology of shared wisdom. This exposure will help them understand the workings of their board or council.

The Shared Wisdom Model

"Whenever you come together, I am with you."

When you come together to break bread, to pray, and to be and to build church, Jesus is with you.

"My Spirit will be with you always."

To each the Lord gives a piece of the wisdom.

To no one does He give all the wisdom of God.

We all get different pieces.

The call of Vatican II

Church belongs to the baptized.

Church is the responsibility of the baptized.

Theology

Our God is the God of the Gathering.

Our God is present to us in many ways.

Our God is present to us in one another.

Implications

We must share our wisdom.

We must hear, respect, and treasure one another's wisdom.

We must work for a climate that is open and respectful.

Stances

>We must be open to new ways of thinking and feeling.
>We must be open to information and data collected by others.
>We must be willing to let go of the need to control.
>We must be willing to let go of the need to win.
>We must be willing to let go of the need to always be right.
>We must be willing to leave the familiar and risk the unfamiliar.

Spirituality

>We must give an obedient response to the Spirit.
>We must be willing to process life by—
>- setting aside prime time to spend with the Lord,
>- finding God space in which to be alone with God, and
>- using an appropriate method for communicating with God.

Leadership

>A pastoral leader is—
>- the spiritual leader,
>- the ecclesial authority, and
>- a member of the group.
>
>A group leader—
>- empowers the members,
>- enables the process, and
>- confronts dysfunctional behavior kindly, clearly, and consistently.

Process

>We must understand the difference in personality types.
>We must learn to use the process skills.
>We must take time for reflective prayer.
>We must take time to gather the wisdom.
>We must learn to accept the discerned decision as the will of the Spirit.

REFLECTION 22
The Philosophy of Shared Wisdom

1. What attitudinal and behavioral changes does the shared wisdom model call you to consider?

_____

_____

_____

_____

2. What structural and behavioral changes does this model call the group to consider?

_____

_____

_____

_____

3. What do you hope will happen as the members of your group come to understand and use the shared wisdom model?

_____

_____

_____

_____

4. What concerns or worries you about adopting the model?

_____

_____

_____

_____

5. What recommendations do you make about your group's possible future?

_____

_____

_____

_____

APPENDIX II
Communal Discernment in the Tradition

As we have seen, the emphasis given to discernment in the early tradition was on personal discernment as a means of personal spiritual growth. There seems little in the early writings after the Council of Jerusalem to indicate the use of discernment for community or group decision making. According to Ann Graff there is some hint of this possibility as early as Origen, however, to be found in the theological anthropology. Reflecting on his insights, she writes:

> ... discernment is seen as a gift and an ability acquired on the path toward God, and that aids one to recognize and follow that path. The possessor of such a gift is gradually able to distinguish with more surety what is of God and what is not. This person learns to distinguish not only what pertains to the relation and direction of his/her own life toward God, but also what characterizes the Christian community. (1)

Saint Benedict, writing his *Rule* in the fifth century, also seems to move in this communal direction when he insists that the entire community be gathered for the sharing of wisdom when decisions need to be made. His reasoning is clear: The abbot is to consult all because the Spirit gives wisdom to all, "even the youngest."

But we have no historical accounts of this communal use of the gift of discernment until Ignatius and his little community of followers were faced with a serious question about their future as a community. That was in 1539, and the process they developed, "The Deliberation," moves the tradition very clearly into the communal experience. It is this process, then, that I wish to pursue, both in terms of its theology and structure and in terms of its implications for the shared wisdom model.

What do we mean by "communal discernment"? John Carroll Futrell says it clearly when he writes:

> Communal spirit discernment is the effort of an entire faith-community to find God and, therefore, to find his actual word here and now to the whole community, to which the whole community as one is called to say "Yes, Father," with one voice. (2)

The goal, then, is to arrive at a "shared decision"—shared both in the input that comes from all the members and in the final acceptance of the decision by all the members.

Since discernment is both a gift and an acquired ability, it calls not only for surrender to the gift of the Spirit but also for the development of a process or method in and through which that gift can be touched and nuanced. Summarizing how these basic concepts were understood and put into practice by Ignatius and his early followers as they worked their way through that first deliberation, Jules Toner notes:

> There are two main parts. The first is taken up with penance, intense prayer, meditation, and Eucharistic liturgy, all in order to attain and maintain purity of heart, freedom of spirit before God and to beg for enlightenment from God. Without purification in adequate measure (who can attain it fully?) and without prayer for God's enlightenment, no one should begin deliberation or long continue in it. The second part of the method is a set of procedures to protect freedom of spirit and mutual openness among the participants while carrying on deliberation, to move the deliberation as smoothly as possible and to bring it to a definite conclusion. (3)

The first thing to be considered, then, is the depth of prayer life to which these men committed themselves. Let it be noticed that they were obviously men of prayer to begin with. It was out of their faith and their ongoing experience of prayer and intimacy with God that they made their decision as recorded in the account of the process:

> In full agreement we settled on this that we would give ourselves to prayer, Masses, and meditations more fervently than usual and, after doing our very best we would for the rest cast all our concerns on the Lord, hoping in him. He is so kind and generous that he never denies his good Spirit to anyone who petitions him in humility and simplicity of heart; rather, he gives all extravagantly, not holding back from anyone. In no way, then, would he who is kindness itself desert us; rather, he would be with us more generously than we asked or imagined. (4)

It is important for us to note that even though Ignatius and his followers agreed to increase their prayer and penance, they did so without limiting their normal apostolic activities. They considered three ways of going about this process. One was to stop all regular ministry and to go away to a place of solitude where they could devote themselves to only this one effort. Another was to commission a few of their number to devote themselves full time to discerning the will of God, with the understanding that all would accept the final decision of the few. Both of these options were rejected. The entire group was to be involved; and that involvement, in terms of personal preparation as well as communal sharing and deliberation, was to be added to the regular and apparently quite demanding schedule of apostolic activity. This historical factor is most helpful to us in our efforts to translate the model for councils and boards, groups typically composed of very active and committed members of the parish and diocese!

Another critical concept is to be found in the shared commitment that held Ignatius and his followers together. In today's church we call an understanding of that commitment a charism or a mission statement. The mission statement expresses the purpose for which the parish or diocese or community exists and serves to focus the group on a unified commitment. It is therefore able to serve as a criterion for decision making while also limiting the possibilities of choices in a positive and healthy way.

Thomas Reese and Paul Roy observe:

> . . . the real challenge to the community is to seek out the presence and the inspiration of the Lord within its life and to make real, human choices of courses of action which will best keep that community alive with the life of God. (5)

But how that life of God touches and forms and challenges that community is related to why that community exists—what it feels itself to be called to, that is, its charism or mission.

Two concerns immediately become evident. The first has to do with the dialectic of community. Here we find that the pre-Vatican theology of church was, in fact, easier to deal with in terms of goals and mission. The church existed for our salvation. She was "to get us to heaven." Institutional goals were not that hard to identify or even to agree on, given that understanding of mission. But Vatican II called us to a church that was to be a community—a living, breathing, struggling people of God with evolving goals. People were to be about caring, worshipping, ministering, journeying together. The dialectic is built into the challenge! We very seldom are brave enough to ask the question, at least out loud or seriously, but that does not make it less important. That question, simply put, is:

What are we to be about—
    a church *being* community or
    a church *doing* ministry?

The answer is not, of course, either/or as much as it must be both/and. Any diocese or parish or religious community must be able to see its ministry flowing from its mission.

Any group wishing to engage in a discerning process or model must have first dealt with this dialectic and come to terms with it in their charism or mission statement. Faith sharing and the sharing of religious values allow decision makers to arrive at mission statements that enable their ministry decisions to be congruent with what they claim to be called to as a community, a parish, or a diocese.

The men working through that first deliberation knew who they were. They had a clear handle on the ministry the Lord had called them to and they shared that understanding. This was the touchstone that provided the criterion for their discerning.

Any council, board, senate, staff, or team desiring to discern a decision or embrace a shared wisdom model must have, it seems to me, something of this same clarity. Futrell says it this way:

> The first prerequisite is communion. That is to say, the members of the community must truly have a consciously shared experience of profound union in a common vocation from the Holy Spirit, which underlies all the differences of opinions and of expressions that make communication so difficult unless all members share the common touchstone core experience of their common charism. Ways must be found, therefore, to bring all members of the community to this experience through a true mutual sharing of faith experiences. . . .
>
> The second prerequisite is common agreement on the basic expression of this communion in words here and now. If we are communally to discern how to realize our profound charismatic communion in community life and apostolic action today, we must use human dialogue as the vehicle of our discernment. In order not to be talking at cross purposes, therefore, it is essential that all are agreed on the basic verbal expression of the communal charism which is the communion of the community, since this is the norm of discernment for all corporate choices. Without this commonly-agreed-upon verbal expression of the norm, the discerners will not be seeking means to the same end. They will simply not be talking about the same thing. (6)

But even given such clarity, a second concern is obvious. We are so very human. We all tend to like our own ideas, opinions, and insights better than anyone else's. Speaking of the reality of this in the early Ignatian group, Toner points out:

> The document quite clearly describes a painful struggle by men of conflicting views trying to find what God wanted all of them to do together. (7)

Nor is there anything magical about the process that dissolves such struggles, as Toner observes when he describes their experience of

> the prolonged, patient effort required in order to reach a conclusion, many days of private prayer, of meditation and reflection, as well as of deliberating together. The profound effort indicates that the earlier tension between conflicting opinions did not easily dissolve. (8)

It seems clear, then, that not only must there be some basic agreement in the group about charism or mission, but there also must be a genuine effort on the part of each participant to arrive at that holy indifference so much a part of the tradition. Individual preparation must lead those who are involved in the discernment experience to a stance of "letting go," allowing God to be God, and to a commitment that will open each to the activity of the Spirit.

In "The Deliberation" three things are identified as the individual preparation that will foster this holy indifference. They are:

1. A commitment to personal prayer, meditation, and sacrifice for the purpose of leading each participant to seek peace and joy in the Spirit

2. A commitment not to discuss the issue with any other participant at this point in the process so as not to be persuaded by each other

3. An effort to consider oneself as an "outsider," that is, not a member of the group, so as to eliminate any vested interests and allow options to be considered only for the greater service of God and the good of all

Some things now become apparent as we pursue "The Deliberation." They include the following:

- The process took place within a community.
- The effort was to develop a further articulation of an already agreed-upon charism.
- The success of the process rested heavily on the discernment of each member.
- There was a high level of trust in God within the group since they had experienced His guidance in the past and had every reason to believe He would continue to be with them in their efforts to serve Him and His people.

Sharing, hearing, and treasuring wisdom was critical at this stage. Toner explains:

> . . . everyone was to form a judgment and to have reasons and to speak to them. Everyone was to be involved, not just a few who were more inclined to urge their views.
>
> Each one's judgment was to be founded on reason, since the decision of the group would be the way of thinking supported by the more powerful reasons. Failure to be clear about what "reasons" are in this context could lead to a number of misunderstandings. (9)

In the process that Ignatius and his followers evolved, they spent the first day of sharing speaking only to the negatives and the second day only to the positives. There is no reason given for starting with the negatives, nor is there anything to lead us to believe that this would always need to be the order followed. However, when you realize that negative responses and reactions often are the result of fear, it seems wise to deal with them first, thus neutralizing the fears and freeing the participants to relate more creatively to the positive aspects of the issue or proposal. What is important in the Ignatian group is that all the wisdom was presented before any discussion or debate took place. Graff observes:

> The design of the conversation which allows separate days to discuss the pros and cons of the matter at issue forestalls precipitant confrontation. Listening to each companion takes place prior to discussion and argument. (10)

And Toner further clarifies:

> This is very different from having some defend one side and some another, each attacking the other's position, and hoping the truth will appear this way. It is even very different from each supporting one side or the other and listening receptively to what the other side has to say. In this method, everyone has to shake himself loose from his prejudgments and any emotional inclinations which dominate his thinking so as to support every alternative *actively* and *sympathetically.* Only after that process is completed is anyone allowed to put the opposing reasons into the balance in order to arrive at even a tentative judgment. (11)

In the Ignatian group each sharing of wisdom, or "gathering of evidence" as Futrell calls it, was followed by prayer and eventually by discussion. There was no apparent effort to struggle against time. They sensed the inappropriateness of programming the Spirit and simply stayed with the process as long as they needed in order to arrive at a discerned decision. Toner observes:

> They did not, however, fall away from the realization of their utter dependence on God with which they had begun. They did not now think that the method they had developed was of any value for finding God's will except insofar as it helped them remain open to the Holy Spirit. They did not think that their own efforts were of any value for finding God's will except insofar as the Holy Spirit, in his overflowing kindness, chose to work through them, leading them to the right judgment. (12)

The difference between unanimity of vote and unanimity of acceptance of a majority vote is explained on pages 50-51. An understanding of this difference is critical to understanding when or if a discerned decision has been reached.

One caution is called for, a caution that comes out of my own lived experience both as a member of a discerning group and as a facilitator working with a discerning group. If my wisdom does not match the final decision, that is *not* to say that I have not heard what the Spirit was saying to me! Futrell says it well:

It is helpful here to recall the fact (clear in the Old Testament and in the two thousand year history of the Church) that the Holy Spirit does not necessarily move individual persons within a community and the community as a whole to the same election at the same time on the same issue. Indeed, he precisely at times moves them to different choices. (13)

The stance I have personally learned to take and have helped others to adopt in this kind of a situation goes like this:

For whatever reason, the Spirit is calling the group to something else than what I am personally discerning. While I do not completely understand or agree with the position, I accept it and affirm it as the will of the Spirit for this group at this time.

I'm not sure if such a stance flows from or is the cause of the peace and joy of heart that are the truest indicators of a discerned decision. But I do know that it is essential to the experience. When, in fact, discernment has happened, all members of the discerning group will be touched by this contentment because they acknowledge in faith the call of the Spirit as being the decision reached. This sense of rightness is the confirmation of the Spirit. It is not an intellectual experience but a feeling. Futrell described it when he writes:

Confirmation of the community election made through the communal discernment will be experienced by all the companions together; *"todos contentos,"* as Ignatius puts it. This shared experience of profound contentment in the Lord bears witness that the members of the community have found God together, and therefore have found his actual word to them as a community here and now. Confirmation is a unanimous experience of the witness of the Holy Spirit. (14)

My experience, however, leads me to a point of disagreement about the unanimity of this feeling of contentment that I believe to be significant. In all the reading I have done on communal discernment, there is an insistence on this unanimous feeling of contentment as being the indicator that a discerned decision has taken place. Very often as I have worked with groups, I have known this to be true and it is, indeed, a beautiful witness!

However, as explained in Chapter 5 (pages 51-53), it is possible for a variety of reasons that an individual member of the group will not be able to accept a decision. When this happens, neither that person nor the group should feel that this inability to surrender to the wisdom of the group represents a failure to discern. There are times when a person simply does not experience the peace and contentment that others in the group clearly experience. But there is also a time to let go of the ideal and live with the reality. Discernment is neither miraculous nor magical. It is a call to simplicity of heart, a willingness to struggle through the journey within the human limitations to be found in one's self and in one another.

Nor is a discerned decision to be seen as final and forever. Life is a dynamic reality. Situations and people and needs change. Toner calls us to this insight when he writes:

> . . . we see that what is God's will in a "mutable decision" can later become a hindrance to God's will and so may need to be brought again to discernment. This turn of events in no way disconfirms or calls into question the conclusion of earlier discernment. It only shows how we have to stay flexible if we are to be always seeking God's will in the flux of human history. (15)

It is that kind of flexibility, of letting go, that enabled Ignatius and his men to reach their historic decision, a decision that graced and gifted the church with the Society of Jesus. Our discerned decisions may not have such dramatic effects, but they will be grace and gift to our parishes, our dioceses, and our communities!

REFERENCE NOTES

CHAPTER 1

1. Alvin J. Lindgren and Norman Shawchuck, *Let My People Go* (Nashville: Abingdon Press, 1980), pp. 9-10.

2. *Lumen Gentium,* 37. All quotations from the Council documents have been taken from *The Conciliar and Post Conciliar Documents,* Austin Flannery, ed. (Northport, N.Y.: Costello Publishing Co., 1975).

3. *Decree on the Apostolate of the Laity,* 1.

4. Ibid., 6.

5. Ibid., 10.

6. James H. Provost, ed., *Code, Community, Ministry* (Washington, D.C.: Canon Law Society of America, 1983), pp. 12-15.

7. Ibid., p. 14.

8. Joan Chittister, *Women, Ministry, and the Church* (New York: Paulist Press, 1983), p. 93.

CHAPTER 2

1. Ernest Larkin, *Silent Presence: Discernment As Process and Problem* (Denville, N.J.: Dimension Books, 1981), p. 6.

2. Ibid., pp. 5, 6, 9, 10.

CHAPTER 3

1. National Council of Catholic Bishops, *Called and Gifted: The American Catholic Laity* (Washington, D.C.: United States Catholic Conference, 1980), p. 3.

2. Claire M. Brissette, *Reflective Living: A Spiritual Approach to Everyday Life* (Whitinsville, Mass.: Affirmation Books, 1983), p. 13.

3. Ibid., pp. 112-13.

CHAPTER 4

1. Paul I. Murphy, *La Popessa* (New York: Warren Books, 1983), p. 101.

2. Joan Ohanneson, *Woman: Survivor in the Church* (Minneapolis: Westminster Press, 1980), p. 23.

3. Matthew Fox, *A Spirituality Named Compassion* (Minneapolis: Winston Press, 1979), pp. 47-50.

4. Ibid., pp. 57-58.

5. Ibid., pp. 66-67.

6. Joan Chittister, "A Feminine Critique of the Peace Pastoral," *Benedictines,* vol. XXXVII, no. 1 (Atchison, Kansas: Mt. St. Scholastica, 1983), pp. 26-30.

CHAPTER 5

1. Jules J. Toner, "A Method for Communal Discernment of God's Will," *Studies in the Spirituality of Jesuits,* vol. III, no. 4 (St. Louis: American Assistancy Seminar on Jesuit Spirituality, 1971), p. 128.

CHAPTER 6

1. John Carroll Futrell, "Learning Leadership from Watershed Down," *Human Development,* vol. 3, no. 4 (New York: Jesuit Education Center for Human Development, 1982), pp. 33-35.

2. Bishop Carroll Dozier, "The Bishop and the Community of the Local Church" (source not available).

3. Provost, *Code,* pp. 79-80.

4. Philip J. Murnion, "Parish Renewal: State(ments) of the Question," *America,* vol. 147 (New York: America Press, 1982), p. 314.

5. Futrell, "Learning Leadership," pp. 33-34.

6. Ibid., p. 34.

CHAPTER 7

1. Richard P. McBrien, *Catholicism,* vol. 2 (Minneapolis: Winston Press, 1980), pp. 980-81.

APPENDIX I

1. Evelyn Eaton Whitehead, *The Parish in Community and Ministry* (New York: Paulist Press, 1978), pp. 46-47.

2. Gerard Egan and Michael Cowan, *People in Systems* (Monterey, Calif.: Brooks/Cole Publishing, 1979), p. 10.

APPENDIX II

1. Ann O'Hara Graff, "Vision of Reality: Discernment and Decision Making in Contemporary Roman Catholic Ecclesiology" (Ph.D. Thesis, University of Chicago Divinity School, 1983), p. 19.

2. John Carroll Futrell, "Communal Discernment: Reflections on Experience," *Studies in the Spirituality of Jesuits,* vol. IV, no. 5 (St. Louis: American Assistancy Seminar on Jesuit Spirituality, 1972), p. 162.

3. Jules J. Toner, "The Deliberation That Started the Jesuits," *Studies in the Spirituality of Jesuits,* vol. VI, no. 4 (St. Louis: American Assistancy Seminar on Jesuit Spirituality, 1974), p. vi.

4. Ibid., p. 186.

5. Thomas J. Reese and Paul J. Roy, "Discernment As Muddling Through," *The Jurist,* vol. XXXI (Washington, D.C.: Department of Catholic Law, Catholic University), p. 86.

6. Futrell, "Communal Discernment," p. 168.

7. Toner, "The Deliberation," p. 182.

8. Ibid., pp. 205-6.

9. Ibid., p. 188.

10. Graff, "Vision of Reality," p. 94.

11. Toner, "The Deliberation," p. 203.

12. Ibid., p. 206.

13. Futrell, "Communal Discernment," p. 165.

14. Ibid., p. 164.

15. Toner, "The Deliberation," pp. 191-92.

SELECTED BIBLIOGRAPHY

Brissette, Claire M. *Reflective Living: A Spiritual Approach to Everyday Life.* Whitinsville, Mass.: Affirmation Books, 1983.

Brissette deals with a spirituality that matches the call to process life, which is so important in a shared wisdom model.

Chittister, Joan. *Women, Ministry, and the Church.* New York: Paulist Press, 1983.

While much of what Chittister writes about is directly related to women religious, there is also a great deal of wisdom in this little book for all of us who are sisters in church. Especially helpful are her insights into the masculine model of church that has dominated for so long.

Fox, Matthew. *A Spirituality Named Compassion.* Minneapolis: Winston Press, 1979.

Fox uses a vocabulary that at first may not seem related to the shared wisdom model. Not so! His experience of ladder skills and his effort to move church to a collaborative model that no longer needs to "climb the ladder" are what makes this book so helpful.

Keating, Charles J. *The Leadership Book.* Rev. ed. New York: Paulist Press, 1982.

This book is devoted to leadership within church models. Especially helpful is the chapter on managing conflict.

Larkin, Ernest. *Silent Presence: Discernment As Process and Problem.* Denville, N.J.: Dimension Books, 1981.

This is a book for personal reflection and prayer. Larkin calls us to be discerning people, recognizing the presence of the Spirit in all of life.

Lindgren, Alvin J., and Shawchuck, Norman. *Let My People Go.* Nashville: Abingdon Press, 1980.

Lindgren and Shawchuck speak out of experience. This is a very practical little book. It gives an overview of church during these days of radical change and then deals with many of the practical skills needed to be part of the movement.

National Council of Catholic Bishops. *Called and Gifted: The American Catholic Laity.* Washington, D.C.: United States Catholic Conference, 1980.

A summary of where the bishops saw the laity of the American church to be and to be going. Enlightening and encouraging.

Ohanneson, Joan. *Woman: Survivor in the Church.* Minneapolis: Westminster Press, 1980.

> Ohanneson gives us history, reality, and future challenge in this book about women and the Catholic church. It is a book for both men and women who struggle with this difficult and painful issue.

Powell, John. *Will the Real Me Please Stand up?* Allen, Texas: Tabor Publishing, 1985.

> Powell collaborates with psychotherapist Loretta Brady to provide twenty-five basic attitudes and practices that will result in effective communication. An extremely practical approach to the communication problems so often experienced in groups as well as between individuals.

Provost, James H., ed. *Code, Community, Ministry.* Washington, D.C.: Canon Law Society of America, 1983.

> The Canon Law Society has done an excellent job of allowing the revised Code to make sense for those involved in parish ministry.

Toner, Jules J. "A Method for Communal Discernment of God's Will," *Studies in the Spirituality of Jesuits,* vol. III, no. 4. St. Louis: American Assistancy Seminar on Jesuit Spirituality, 1971.

> Toner is a scholar of the discernment process. This publication is, therefore, a scholarly approach to the tradition of discernment. It provides many important insights for the application of the tradition to the shared wisdom model.